CHOICES

Books by Frederic F. Flach, M.D.

CHOICES: Coping Creatively with Personal Change

THE SECRET STRENGTH OF DEPRESSION

CHOICES

Coping Creatively with Personal Change

Frederic F. Flach, M.D.

J. B. Lippincott Company

Philadelphia and New York

Published by arrangement with Bantam Books, Inc.

U.S. Library of Congress Cataloging in Publication Data

Flach, Frederic F
  Choices : coping creatively with personal change.

  Bibliography: p.
  Includes index.
   1. Personality change.   2.   Stress (Psychology).
3.   Creative ability.   I.   Title.
BF698.2.F57   158'.1   77-22923
ISBN-0-397-01234-9

TO MY EDWARDIAN PARENTS,
whose courage and imagination enabled them
to live with meaning
in the strange and bewildering second half
of the twentieth century

Contents

Author's Note

In preparing this manuscript I deliberately attempted to employ the very principles of creative thought that I was setting out to describe, such as preparation through study and plenty of simmering to let ideas take shape. As a result, even though it is "finished," I am left with the distinct feeling that it is not finished. And of course it could not be. New insights come to mind so that one is continually being led down the endless corridors of new possibilities. I have no doubt, for example, that one of the reasons I found it hard at times to order certain concepts was the fact that the subjects I was writing about—the ability to be creative, a capacity for insight, a healthy response to stress—are not just interrelated processes but in fact are reflections of one and the same process, a kind of life principle. And in such matters, the final word is never in.

Accordingly, I must acknowledge the restraint, the insistence on clarity, and of course the invaluable enthusiasm that my editors, Grace Bechtold, Beatrice Rosenfeld, and

9

Wilhemina Marvel, brought to my efforts. We had worked together before, on *The Secret Strength of Depression*. This second time around only confirmed my faith in the importance of the balance and personal interaction required for many creative endeavors to work well.

CHOICES

1
Why Choices?

Most people can look back over the years and identify a time and place at which their lives changed significantly. Whether by accident or design, these are the moments when, because of a readiness within us and a collaboration with events occurring around us, we are forced to seriously reappraise ourselves and the conditions under which we live and to make certain choices that will affect the rest of our lives.

For me, one such change was triggered in 1959 by reading a rather complex and irritatingly abstract book called *The Phenomenon of Man*. The author, Pierre Teilhard de Chardin, was a French Jesuit, a paleontologist, and a visionary. He was also an evolutionist who developed a concept of the universe and man's place in it that has proved astonishingly prophetic.

Teilhard de Chardin's theory was that because of a progressive enlargement in man's consciousness and an increase in human contact—the result of many factors, but basically of more people on earth and less space—the direction of man's evolution had shifted away from physical adaptation to an evolution that was more psychological and social in nature.

Reading *The Phenomenon of Man* set the stage for a major transition in my thinking. I turned away from the traditional view of mental and emotional disturbances as a failure on the part of the individual to cope with his environment, and began to consider falling apart to be the only healthy response for a human being to have when confronted with certain kinds of life stresses.

This book also catalyzed a change in the way I regarded psychotherapy itself. Until then I had looked on psychoanalysis, psychotherapy, or various forms of biological treatment primarily as methods to relieve suffering patients of their pain and restore them to a so-called normal level of function.

Suddenly—and it was suddenly—I could see how increasing awareness need not be simply a therapeutic tool, but a goal in itself. Even though the process was often painful, if properly handled it would eventually give patients the ingredients for a better way to live and cope, enlarging the scope of their personal freedom, improving their ability to make choices and their responsiveness to change. Applying Teilhard's concepts on an individual scale, it was possible to see a person's whole life as a process of psychological evolution, ideally an upward and forward movement, although one that would be interrupted at times by plateaus and periods of coming apart.

The wall between mental health and mental illness dissolved somewhat. I began to consider new ways to look at problems that as a psychiatrist I encountered every day. In my relationships with patients I found myself forfeiting the "I'm OK, you're not OK" assumption that our culture and my training had encouraged and beginning to take a more positive view of what they were experiencing.

A second important insight from Teilhard de Chardin accompanied this more personal one. Whatever insecurities we might feel in our own immediate lives were being enormously reinforced by the evolutionary crisis that the world itself was going through. With the social values and institutions to which we had once been able to look for support apparently vanishing before our eyes, each of us would often be faced with the necessity of dealing with moments of personal confusion very much alone.

Looking back, I now see that my encounter with the thinking of Teilhard de Chardin was one of those intense creative moments when we painfully disengage from one way of viewing things and shift to new ground. Such an experience, of course, demands an openness to new ideas and situations. It also requires a period of dissatisfaction with the knowledge and attitudes that we already hold. It presupposes curiosity, a certain hunger for change, and a willingness to take risks, and it is far more likely to occur when we are unhappy or dissatisfied with the way things are.

I had been disenchanted with the field of psychiatry for some time. I could not understand the rigid refusal of psychiatrists to take a more flexible and well-rounded approach to the diagnosis and treatment of patients. Why, I kept asking, did those who were committed to certain psychological schools of thought seem unable to comprehend the importance of biological forces in human behavior? Why did those who were convinced that behavior was rooted in the biochemistry of the brain find it so hard to consider that the person's relation to the environment was also important? Psychiatrists seemed estranged from one another, divided into camps, and singularly resistant to new ideas. Nor were these questions merely academic; they had a direct bearing on the quality of care that patients were receiving.

For a number of years, my own research had been devoted to the study of biological factors in schizophrenia and depression, specifically the role of the thyroid gland and of calcium metabolism. Gradually the problem of depression emerged as my main focus. At first, I considered all depression as a form of illness. But as I began to understand more about the complex psychological, environmental, and biological factors involved, I became convinced that the real problem for men and women experiencing depression was often not the fact that they were depressed. Instead, the central issue was their inability to experience depression directly, to learn from it, and to recover from it. There were often plenty of reasons for these people to be depressed—divorce, the death of someone in the family, financial reverses, all sorts of significant losses. But they did not seem able to adapt to these changes successfully in a reasonable period of time, because they were unable either to fall apart emotionally when such losses occurred or, if they did, to pull themselves together again.

I began to think of this phenomenon as a lack of resilience. Ideally, the human being should possess a kind of resilience factor, a shock-absorber system, that permits him or her to respond to change with a period of psychological distress which is followed by recovery and which should, in fact, be an enriching experience in itself. Beyond the boundaries of medicine, this was by no means a new concept. It was as old as man's history. St. John of the Cross described the essential "dark night of the soul" that preceded the achievement of new levels of spiritual perfection.

Coincidence plays a major role in the evolution of our thinking. At about that time I became a close friend of the late psychoanalyst Lawrence Kubie. Stimulated by our discussions, I read his monograph on creativity, which pointed to the unconscious as a source of original ideas. Then I read Arthur Koestler's rather complex examination of the creative process and from there moved on to more recent studies of creativity. Much to my surprise, I realized that my own thoughts about resilience and these descriptions of creativity overlapped. In fact, they were practically identical.

Resilence Is Creativity

Again and again, I found creativity defined as a psychological process and as that faculty of the personality which enables us to replace old perceptions with new ones or to combine old ideas in new ways. This is essentially what happens in psychotherapy when patients gain insight or change their behavior.

It required some effort on my part to grasp this broader definition of creativity. Until then, like many people, I had thought of creativity as restricted to art and science. I had also been misled by the popular misconception that links creativity to instability. I had often heard colleagues describe an associate who was always late for appointments, had a terrible temper, behaved eccentrically, made excessive demands on other people, and could never be counted on to have his manuscripts in on time for publication as probably being creative because he was so irresponsible. The extensive and solid research into the nature of creativity has actually revealed the very opposite. Those qualities observed among creative individuals that seem directly connected with their creativity are identical to those found among the most psychologically healthy people: for example, flexibility, and the capacity to integrate concepts that seem on the surface to be contradictory.

My exhilaration at realizing that creativity might be related to mental health and the ability to cope was tempered by another consideration. Our society, characteristically, has packaged, sold, and consumed "creativity" in such a way that its dignity, its value, and even its practical relevance to day-to-day life have been compromised. The very word provokes, at one and the same time, a reaction of hope and a sense of fraudulence. We have heard too much about creative sex, creative cooking, creative divorce, creative fighting.

Nonetheless, as I probed more and more into the work on creativity, seeing how the structure of the creative process had been analyzed by scientists, such as the German physicist Hermann von Helmholtz and the French mathematician Henri Poincaré, as well as more recently by such behavioral scientists as Morris Stein and E. Paul Torrance and psychiatrist Anthony Storr, I became convinced that I was on the right track. My resilience construct was confirmed again and again. The creative process, it became clear, involved disruption and recovery. Like depression, it hurt temporarily, and the source of this pain was rooted both in the need to disengage, to forfeit something valued and familiar, and in the confusion of being without moorings, without direction, thrown off balance, on the way toward something new and often quite unpredictable.

In addition, the process itself had been divided into four specific stages, and by thoroughly mastering these stages, one could learn to cultivate one's own creativity through practice.

Stages in The Creative Process

Since creative breakthroughs do not float in out of the void but are usually preceded by long periods of intentional, determined, disciplined thinking, the first stage was designated as *preparation*, or saturation with one's subject.

However, when one has recognized that there is a problem to be solved or an opportunity to be grasped, it may not be possible to deal with the situation immediately. No answers come, or the first set of answers are simply inadequate or so conventional as to be useless. By settling for an early conclusion, or by going over and over the issue in an effort to bludgeon a way to a solution, one may fail to reach the point in the creative process at which truly new insights occur.

Hence the second stage in the process is that of *incubation*: the period during which one puts the matter aside and lets it "simmer" out of consciousness. This was the step in the creative process that I personally found most difficult, since my natural inclination is to get things settled in a hurry. Yet unless one allows an incubation period for an unpredictable length of time—a few days, a few weeks or months, sometimes even years—it is often impossible to discover original points of view, since the connections that have to be made can be made only within the unconscious mind. This kind of waiting has nothing to do with the all-too-human tendency to procrastinate. Rather, it is an active psychological process, and the more I practiced it in looking for solutions, the shorter I found the incubation period becoming.

The third stage is *illumination*, the moment when new possibilities begin to break into consciousness, whether these are answers to seemingly unsolvable scientific inquiries, the resolution of some highly charged personal dilemma, or a sudden flash of insight during psychotherapy.

The fourth and final stage was called *verification*, the process by which the new idea is put into practice and tested to see if it works.

Although I was gratified to realize that there were principles and techniques one could use to increase one's ability to approach problems creatively, I was still troubled by their somewhat mechanical quality. There was, it seemed to me, a difference between employing creative methods to deal with particular situations and becoming a more creative person—one who has learned to live creatively. At critical moments in life, when major changes occurred and one was faced with the need to make significant choices, a creative person would almost instinctively respond by falling back a bit and then moving forward again with renewed energy and a fresh point of view. To some degree I found that this problem could be solved cumulatively, through experience. In other words, the more one learned about how to consider options effectively and choose the most suitable of them, the more spontaneously creative one would become.

The Stress Connection

But there was yet another aspect. My exploration of the creative process had begun in the context of reconsidering the nature of depression and psychological health. The role that stress played in this matter was central to my thinking. As a student, I had been impressed by Dr. Hans Selye's pioneering research on the nature of stress, and it not only reinforced my choice of psychiatry as a field but encouraged me to pursue my psychobiological research. I had always known that many illnesses of a physical nature—heart disease, for example, and migraine headache—were caused, at least in part, by a failure to cope adequately with stress. I also knew that stress plays a similar role in many psychiatric conditions as well. Suddenly I could see a clear and definitive relationship between creativity on the one hand and the ability to cope with stress on the other.

It suddenly struck me that the steps involved in the creative process were practically identical to those involved in the human being's healthy response to stress, particularly to the kind of stress that demands personal change. By definition, stress implies a shift in the individual's equilibrium and requires him to regain his balance afterward. Creativity required the same sequence of events. Moreover, creativity was itself a very stressful experience.

I began to see that patients suffering with psychosomatic disorders not only lacked the ability to recover after the impact of stress but were even unable to respond appropriately to stress by becoming emotionally upset and, to a certain extent, falling apart. Patients suffering with psychiatric conditions such as chronic depression, having decompensated in the face of stress, were then unable to pull themselves together again. If one could learn, therefore, to respond creatively to stress, the chances of a healthier and more fulfilling life increased immensely.

The lives of all of us have been or will be marked by disruptions in the balance established within ourselves and between ourselves and our worlds. There are periods of intense stress when we must make important choices about ourselves that will affect us for the rest of our lives. What form these take will be determined by the kind of lives we are leading. "In quiet, uneventful lives, the changes internal and external are so small," wrote the English author Samuel Butler, in *The Way of All Flesh*, "that there is little or no strain in the process of fusion and accommodation; in other lives there is great strain, but there is also great fusing and accommodating power. A life will be successful or not, accordingly as the power of accommodation is equal or unequal to the strain of fusing and adjusting internal and external changes."

This power to fuse and accommodate which Butler described is indeed creativity. That was in 1885. Today fewer and fewer people find their lives quiet and uneventful. Changes take place at an accelerated pace and touch everyone in some way. In a world of increasingly complex stresses, personal and cultural, we can no longer afford to use our creative abilities only to solve specific problems here and there. Our health and our sanity require that we learn how to live lives that are genuinely creative.

2
The Kind of Stress
That Makes Us Change

The concerns that affect all of us today are not difficult to identify; the cover of the *Reader's Digest* says it all: saving our marriages, restoring our sexual potency, keeping our blood pressure down and our spirits up, recovering from the impact of the death of someone we love, coping with the rising cost of living, combatting the erosion of our cities and our environment in general, overcoming loneliness, discovering personal significance to our lives. Every time we pick up a magazine or turn on the television set we are reminded, in harrowing detail, of the stresses we face, of what might go wrong if it hasn't already.

The United States has become a stress-conscious nation, anxiety-ridden, in search of formulas. This is partly the result of affluence, which has provided physical comforts but not the health and peace of mind to enjoy them. It is also the outcome of an extended life span; there is more time to be alive, and so there is more reason to worry about the quality of the added years. Less trapped by work,

we have more free time in which to do—what? Much of
our energy has been focused on keeping ourselves physically fit, but quite a bit of attention has now begun to
overflow into keeping ourselves mentally fit as well. And
so we have become seriously concerned with the problem
of stress and how to prevent it from doing us irrevocable
damage.

Stress is no longer a word with a remote academic aura.
In the age of "future shock," it has become a familiar, if
unwelcome, presence in our lives. To cope with it, we
have turned more and more to the new behavioral sciences, raiding them in search of ways to increase self-awareness and of psychological weapons to ward off problems
or deal with them more effectively. Encounter groups and
transactional analysis, meditation and alpha wave control,
sex therapy and the human potential movement are but a
few examples of a rather haphazard effort to apply the find-
ings of an infant science to the solution of the everyday
problems with which we are all faced. Millions of people
have taken a plunge into one or more of these experiences—some emerging with only skepticism and disillu-
sionment, others with a superficial sense of well-being that
dissipates within a few weeks, still others with a feeling of a
genuine and exhilarating breakthrough in self-knowledge
and insight.

While many of these specific approaches may not even
be in our vocabulary a few years from now, the overall
trend to greater personal awareness is far more than a fad.
It acknowledges and reflects the undercurrent of uneasiness that most of us feel, the sense that we are no longer
in sufficient control of things, that we are entitled to get

more out of life than we do, and that we now have to work harder to find what used to be taken for granted—a sense of direction. In addition, this trend stems from the frequency with which people are faced with major stresses that call for personal change.

Hans Selye defined stress as any kind of stimulus—physical, psychological—that tampers with the equilibrium of the organism, from the smallest cell to the entire human being. The connotations of the term "stress" have generally been negative; we tend to overlook the fact that any kind of change within us and within our environment—good as well as bad—is the stuff that stress is made of.

The Response to Stress

There is an intimate and reciprocal connection between stress and personal change. Stress forces growth, and gaining the insight necessary for growth is in itself stressful. In dealing with any kind of stress, there are basically three stages that must be recognized: its impact; the imbalance produced by that impact; and the process of recovery, or putting the pieces together again.

First there is the impact. A husband turns to his wife after fifteen years of what she considered a fundamentally good marriage and tells her that he is no longer interested in continuing it. A long-time employee discovers through the grapevine that he is no longer in favor at work and that those in charge have been holding important, decision-making conferences without inviting him to attend.

Whether stressful situations are acute, immediate, and of short duration or stretch over a period of years—an unhappy love affair or unsatisfactory work situation—the net effect is the second stage, an imbalance in the biological and psychological systems of the person experiencing it. It is an imbalance most often felt in emotional terms: anxiety, fear, panic, anger, a chronic sense of helpless frustration, and futility. If the stress is an immediate and sudden one, the feelings are often numbed temporarily, permitting one to carry on in a rational and purposeful manner until the critical conditions settle down. Afterward, regardless of how the dilemma is resolved, the full reaction is felt and one tends to fall apart.

The third phase in the normal response to stress involves a natural healing process. A strong urge to restore equilibrium exists after that equilibrium has been upset by stress. There is a very important distinction, however, between the kind of stressful experience that calls for a restoration of things to the condition they were in before and the kind that demands a new and quite different kind of balance afterward. If your hand becomes infected, all that is necessary is for your body to fight the infection successfully so that you have a healthy hand again, not a hand in any way different from the way it was before. By contrast, certain kinds of stresses require you to emerge from them changed in some way. They literally force you to form new viewpoints and, in the process, to extinguish or let go of old ones.

When I was twenty-three, I spent a summer in Havana studying tropical medicine. One afternoon another student and I went sailing. A sudden gust of wind capsized the boat and we could not right it. We drifted all night for thirty miles along the coast, never knowing whether our half-submerged boat would sink and fully aware that, in shark-infested waters, we could never swim the mile to shore. We were rescued the next morning. But nothing could ever be the same again. Until then, I had shared the common belief of youth that I was very much in control of my life. Afterward, the profound role that fate, or chance, or whatever you choose to call it, plays in life was indelibly impressed upon me.

In everyday life, success and failure alike inevitably produce a complex state of stress, demanding that we reappraise ourselves at many levels. This reappraisal is a necessary step in recovering from defeat, but it is also necessary in adjusting to success. Success means not only that we must resolve the depression that accompanies the loss of an old purpose no longer relevant, but that we must reconsider who we are and what we are about at this point in our lives in order to locate new directions to move in. And as we do so, we will emerge irrevocably different.

There are many other stressful experiences that force us to emerge from them with a significantly changed way of looking at ourselves; one example is being single again after a divorce and giving up the sense of being married which may have become so much a part of our identity that it takes months, sometimes years, to feel comfortable in the new condition.

The Changing Nature of Stress

There is nothing new about stress itself, but the character of stress—the elements which compose it—can change and in the last century have changed radically. The major characteristics of contemporary stress are its psychological and social nature, the rate at which it takes place, and its unpredictability.

Death and disease, obviously, are still with us, but they have acquired a somewhat more remote quality. People live longer nowadays, and many do not encounter the loss of parents, brothers, sisters, lovers during the early years of their lives. This results in an unhealthy prolongation of the sense of omnipotence—"I can do anything; I will go on forever"—which a child commonly feels and which, in previous generations, was corrected at an earlier age by a confrontation with the reality of death.

Such a condition sets the stage for unrealistic expectations, which are reinforced by a consumer-oriented economy. As we adopt a "more is better" philosophy, we focus more on what is wrong in our lives rather than on what is right about them. What is missing becomes the central theme.

The kinds of stress that are likely to preoccupy us now are far more complex and considerably less tangible. One kind is created by a preoccupation with economic security. Although poverty and starvation are still widespread throughout the world, Western man views economic security primarily as a matter of consumer power and a scale of status significance. Money has become a symbol of one's worth, and the threat of not having "enough"—however much "enough" is—can actually jeopardize one's self-esteem.

Competition, a normal spur to motivation, seems to have run amuck, infiltrating all kinds of organizations, often subtly but in a no less deadly way, by molding an atmosphere in which insecurity abounds despite the fact that the rewards of victory are often without much substance and that achieving them frequently triggers a need in the person who "wins" to self-destruct.

Although concern about acceptance and rejection has always been normal, the fear of being rejected by other people and the anguish we experience when we are rejected, or at least when we believe ourselves to be rejected, has become more intense and more likely to be taken as a serious sign of personal failure. This reflects a significant change in values to a unique emphasis on the quality of interpersonal relationships.

"I knew our marriage wasn't working, that we weren't good for each other. I antagonized him. He stifled me," commented one woman faced with the end of a marriage that had lasted over twenty years. "I wanted out, to feel free to breathe again. So I didn't understand why I hurt so much, or why I can't bear the thought of his marrying again. It's as if *he* rejected me. God, it's complicated."

Complicated is the word. For instead of being simple, readily perceived and understood, and easily met, contemporary stress is much more complex, since it involves the more intangible qualities usually associated with the human being's appraisal of himself and his relationship to others. It is one thing to lose someone you love because he dies. It is quite another to lose someone you love because he does not want to be with you any more, especially when you are aware of the many forces operating within each of you that led to this rejection.

Freedom of choice can provide additional stress. When we are free to marry, divorce, and remarry, free to change our work, free to change the place and the style of our living almost at will, this kind of mobility produces an enormous amount of anxiety. For it is on ourselves that the responsibility for the consequences of our choices must be placed. And this is especially true when the particular role which we have assumed for ourselves is in danger of being shattered.

During the last decade, the women's liberation movement, formally and informally, has called women's attention to the fact that they must find new roles for themselves in a changing society. Being a mother and a wife may not be enough. On the surface, this is a simple and legitimate concern. But as it is experienced by millions of men and women, it is a most serious stress, hitting the very core of their identities.

Harold Green was a fifty-five-year-old patient of mine. He was angry, threatened, and confused by a letter he had received from his wife, Marion, who had been visiting her mother in Chicago and had decided not to return home for a month. He read the letter aloud bitterly, punctuating it with his own comments and reactions:

> "Dearest Harry,
> "I feel very secure in our love for each other, but not very secure about the prospects for our future together. Primarily because that future is based on the past, and I am afraid of returning to the old patterns. The old patterns mean living under conditions that are ultimately suitable to you, but not to me. ["What the hell is she talking about?"]
> "We were never honest with each other. You hold things inside, because you don't want any trouble. I have to be careful of everything I say. If I'm critical, you take it personally and get angry. ["How else am I supposed to

take it when she says that I've made her life miserable for thirty years?"]

"More important, since I've been here, I have realized that I really am a normal person. I've learned to deal with my conflicts. I understand my ups and downs. Being what I am and the way that I am has contributed to this dilemma. Still, I have started to feel that your response to me and the total unwillingness you've had to consider my need to be what I am are the things that set off my depression. My love and sensitivity to you have always left me open to being manipulated.

"I still need to love, but my need to give has been replaced by the need to share. ["Now she's accusing me of not sharing!"]. We can't rely on the past to solve today's problems. Love doesn't conquer all; if it did, we wouldn't be faced with this sense of incompatibility ["That does it!"]

"I have no answers, only questions. Why have you kept me like a small child—always wanting to be dependent on you? ["I can't tell you how often I encouraged her to get out and do things on her own. Sure, when the kids were small, I thought she ought to stay home. But so did she, then."] Is that what you want me to come back to?

"I have no faith in the fact that I can please you anymore when I am truly being myself. And I have to be myself! No more old me! This is the struggle that has been going on a long time, my need to be me, and your need to stop that growth. How can we build a relationship on that premise? No way!

"Today is the first day of the rest of my life. Strangely, I still love you. Marion."

Harold Green turned to me and asked: "What is she talking about? We had a great marriage, three great kids. I love her. I never wanted to block her from being herself, developing her talents. She's really very talented. But this is tearing me apart. It's been building up for a couple of years. Just when we're ready to enjoy life she pulls this kind of thing. She used to *like* my being strong. She liked the fact that I could make decisions, where to live, where to send the kids to school. Now she wants something different. How can I change? I don't even know what she wants."

Perplexing, bewildering social changes and value shifts take place within the framework of a high degree of personal anxiety and suggestibility. There is no way to estimate how many women were influenced by an article in *New York* magazine written by a woman who left her husband and children in Baltimore and came to the "big city" to find excitement in a career as a copy-editor and fulfillment in new sexual and romantic encounters. When there is no common ethic—when the various segments of society cannot agree on a few definitive rights and wrongs— the resulting ambiguity leaves every individual highly vulnerable to every new formula that seems to offer relief from distress and anxiety or a new kind of joy that is generally rather ill defined. Worse yet, when there is little consensus about what is best for the individual or for society, there is a strong tendency to resort to the rule of force. "What's in it for me?" has become a common yardstick, with manipulation and abuse so much the norm that we have even developed schools of psychological self-defense, such as systematic assertive therapy, to protect ourselves.

At the same time there is a general unstructuring in the traditional institutions of society—the family, the church, the university, the government. The events of Watergate can only be seen as the proverbial top of the iceberg; they revealed not just a few dishonest men who violated the laws and ethics of our society, but men who rose to power and influence precisely because we have created a climate in which a ruthless kind of leadership can flourish.

We also cannot help being affected by the demise of a world that emphasized personal accountability and told us that we were masters of our own fate. Sigmund Freud and B. F. Skinner have unwittingly conspired to make self-determination obsolete. Freud's theories, with their insistence on the formative significance of the first six years of life, are as widely opposed to Skinner's behaviorism as possible, except, ironically, with regard to one point: the lack of free choice. Their thinking has infiltrated the novels, films, and school systems of the country with the sweep of a McDonald's food chain, carrying with it the message that what and who we are is the result either of a childhood over which we had no control or of conditioning experiences that have been forced upon us.

The helplessness induced by such influences is intensified by the loss of a sense of continuity—historical or personal. When Marion Green stated in her letter to Harold that the future could not be based on the past, she was pointing to her feeling of a major break in the continuum of her life, a feeling increasingly familiar to each of us. The cause: the rapid rate at which changes take place, and the fact that these changes are not just technologic, economic, or geographic but in fact highly personal. I have not seen the home where I grew up for over twenty years. Once, five years ago, I was within a few miles of it, on a parkway. I almost turned off, but didn't, as if it would be too painful, and somehow too confusing, to do so. So much has changed since that it would jar the senses to be immediately confronted with the distance between two points in time.

Anyone who has been through divorce knows what this feeling is like. Anyone who has been through a major religious experience, either conversion or disenchantment, knows what it is like. It is a major disconnection between the person who was, with all that surrounded him to identify him to himself and his world, and the person he has become over the course of a series of disruptive events. What could be more disorienting than to be separated, once and for all, from the guidelines and the associations of the past, including the very person one then felt oneself to be?

Primarily psychological and social, complex and intangible, occurring against the background of social confusion and unstable value systems, the stresses we must cope with appear to be especially characteristic of a relatively educated and free society. When Skinner advocates abandoning freedom and dignity in favor of conditioning and regimentation, he is really taking what some might consider a highly practical approach to a variety of human problems. For the removal of options is a guaranteed way of reducing anxiety, temporarily at least, since anxiety can be removed by absolutes. A setting in which messages and signals are unclear is one in which anxiety will flourish.

Highly structured, more totalitarian forms of society are probably not caught up in the kind of stresses experienced in more democratic nations, or at least not yet. However, if, as Teilhard de Chardin proposed, these stresses are an inherent part of an evolutionary expansion in consciousness and human interrelatedness, it is only a matter of time before those societies begin to feel the same pressures.

Moreover, contemporary stress is characterized by the fact that our own personal, intimate experiences of stress— at home, at work—occur against a background of changes of such magnitude that we cannot fully comprehend them or even admit to their significance. Overshadowed by the racial turbulence throughout the world, the events in Southeast Asia, economic crises with simultaneous inflation and recession, the energy dilemma, the revelation of crime in high government positions, the most threatening single event of the past decade may well have been the arrival of human beings on the moon. Prepared for this event by science fiction, and having grown curiously accustomed to spectacular scientific breakthroughs, we have become somewhat hardened to the idea of new discoveries. We expect them and therefore underestimate their potential impact. Standing in the London airport when the moon landing was televised, I was reminded of a passage from John Steinbeck's *Log from the Sea of Cortez* which describes a frog in a mountain cleft finding a cigarette butt and trying to decide just how to handle this discovery without admitting the existence of man—without allowing himself to imagine an order of things which is different from the order he already knows.

> The tree-frog in the high pool in the mountain cleft, had he been endowed with human reason, on finding a cigarette butt in the water might have said, "Here is an impossibility. . . . Here is evidence of fire and there has

been no fire. This thing cannot fly nor crawl nor blow in the wind. In fact, this thing cannot be and I will deny it, for if I admit that this thing is here the whole world of frogs is in danger. . . ." And so that frog will for the rest of his life try to forget that something that is, is.

3
Turning Points
in Life

In the course of a lifetime, there are a number of points at which we encounter major changes in the patterns of our lives. In adult years, these transition points are not hard to identify in advance, yet somehow they always seem to come upon us by surprise. Like Steinbeck's frog, we would often prefer to close our eyes to their significance.

Characteristic of most turning points is the fact that psychological, biological, and environmental changes all happen simultaneously. In the mid-forties, for instance, one is confronted with children leaving home, with placing parents in nursing homes, with reconsidering one's career direction and economic future, with sensing the changes in one's hormonal balance, with perceiving the suddenly rapid passage of the years.

The Anatomy of a Turning Point

Getting married is another significant turning point. Once the decision to marry is made, something happens to each person. It is true that the general quality of the relationship between a man and woman before marriage is likely to be a fairly accurate indication of the kind of interaction they will have afterward. If they bicker and argue a great deal before, there is little likelihood that they will cease to do so because they have signed a contract. If one or the other is extremely unreliable, capricious in love, or undependable with money, it is unlikely that this will change, and one of the most erroneous assumptions with which people enter marriage is that one will be able to change the person one marries once the relationship is legalized.

Even when the relationship seems fine before getting married—sexually, in terms of shared interests, closeness—certain vital insights must be acquired if the marriage is going to work well and if the previous compatibility is to survive. Almost without exception and regardless of how long the couple may have known each other or lived together, getting married is bound to activate innumerable environmental problems and inner psychological difficulties. On a fairly simple level, for example, in-laws will react in a new way toward the person who has now become part of the family and is therefore entitled to receive whatever consideration or abuse the family is accustomed to delivering.

In addition, there is the fear of loss of freedom. The act of marrying entails a commitment. In spite of the frequency of divorce, few people marry expecting to separate, and commitment, by definition, involves a limit on one's freedom. Being committed can be experienced as being trapped unless one has clarified in one's own mind how to enter into a sharing relationship without forefeiting a basic sense of individuality. This conflict cannot be resolved through elaborate contracts or a division of specific responsibilities following a pattern similar to labor-management negotiations, as is sometimes suggested. It requires, instead, insight and a careful redefinition of oneself in terms of the new situation.

On a deeper level, something else takes place when two people marry. The attitudes which men and women have toward the person they marry have been found to be strongly affected by the kind of relationship each partner has had with his or her mother. Furthermore, within each person there is a conflict between establishing the kind of marriage that he or she consciously wants and re-establishing the kind of family life that has been imprinted within his or her unconscious during childhood by the character of the relationships existing within the home at that time. On an unconscious level, there may be an assumption, rooted in the model of what things were like growing up, that either husband or wife is to be dominant, and dominating. Unless both partners have sufficient insight into this force and the ability to modify it, it can steadily, insidiously, disrupt the initial balance of the marriage.

Childhood impressions also affect adult perceptions. That a man's perception of his wife will probably be colored by the sort of woman his mother was is not surprising. It is not so widely recognized that a wife's perception of her husband is also influenced by the kind of relationship she had with her mother.

"My mother was always critical, never seemed to appreciate anything I did," a woman patient told me. "I tried hard to please her, but I never could. I bend over back-ward to please my husband, and I don't seem to be able to succeed with that either. I used to love him and enjoy being with him. Now sometimes I even hate him. Most of the time I feel smothered by him, or just a failure."

In fact, this particular woman's husband was quite un-critical and appreciative. "It's true," he observed, "the more she says I don't appreciate her, the harder it gets to say it or even feel it. Sometimes I feel as though I'm being pulled into a role which isn't me, one I don't want to play, just to satisfy some need of hers."

In the same way, the nature of the relationship between the parents of both partners serves as an unconscious model that may shift the equilibrium of the marriage.

"The balance of power in my family rested with my mother," said one woman, "and in my husband's family it was held tightly by his father. Neither of us wants to repeat that kind of pattern, but we have found ourselves increas-ingly caught up in power struggles over crazy kinds of is-sues, threatening each other with 'If you do this, I'll do that' and long spells of just not talking to each other."

The parental model will be activated especially by the birth of children—another major turning point at which the need for insight is critical. In each of us, the experi-ence of becoming a parent reinforces whatever identifica-tion with our own parents we have formed, even if we have long since forgotten or struggled to abandon it. A man whose father was tyrannical may become, defen-sively, overly permissive. A woman whose mother was overly indulgent and incapable of setting limits on her children may unwittingly treat her own children the same way without being aware of it, often deluding herself into thinking that she is quite an effective disciplinarian. If confronted with this discrepancy by her husband or anyone else, she may adamantly deny it.

Behavioral scientists have observed that most people tend to raise their children in the same way in which they were raised, for better or worse, deliberately or unwittingly. There is no doubt in my mind that much of the anxiety and overconcern which American parents have about being a parent—hardly beneficial to the children—stems from a failure to come to terms with this very conflict. Instead, people remain trapped by the link between their own way of doing things and their parents' way, unable to arrive at their own estimate of the kind of parents they want to be.

You can predict stress, in essence, when you marry and when you have children, in spite of the fact that normally both are occasions for joy. It is the kind of stress that demands not only an increase in awareness of forces within yourself, but also the power to tolerate a period of disequilibrium and to recover from it with new insight. When the inherent stress of the situation is not recognized for what it really is—a demand for creativity and change—it can readily be misinterpreted as resulting from something basically wrong with the marriage and can lead to a disruption of closeness and communication that makes recovery nearly impossible.

Understanding Change

Other, equally significant turning points in life call for a similar capacity for insight and change because they force people to revise the way in which they experience themselves. One is reaching middle age. The stresses of middle age have been discussed again and again, and still they usually come as a shock. They happen to other people, not to us. The impact of children growing up, for example, stimulates within us memories and feelings that correspond to the conditions of our own lives when we were their age. An increase in sexual desire and sudden involvements in extramarital affairs by men and women in their forties are motivated to a significant degree by the sexual coming of age of their own children. Impulsive, immature behavior in middle-aged people is often activated by the mere presence of teenagers in the home. Much has been said about the identification of the child with the parent, but rarely does one consider the reverse—the strong identification that exists for the parent with the child.

I can remember standing in the airport saying good-by to one of my sons on his way to Wyoming to work on a ranch for the summer. It was the first time he had left home to go any distance for any length of time. He was seventeen. Suddenly I remembered my own father standing in the old Pennsylvania Railroad Station in New York, before it was torn down to make room for the new Madison Square Garden. He was saying good-by to me. I was going off to basic training in the Navy, and it was my first real separation from home. The memory set off a strong wave of sadness, yet at the same time a sense of joy that stemmed from a feeling of closeness and identity with my own son at that moment.

At life's turning points, past and present fuse. The recent emphasis on living in the "now" may reduce some of the anxiety we feel about not having much control over the future; it may also free some of us from unpleasant associations of the past. However, to the degree that it cuts us off from our own personal history, it does us a tremendous disservice, causing us to feel disconnected and perpetually adrift. Recalling the past can prepare us to deal with the stresses and experiences of life in a more conscious and intentional way and so diminish the influence of hidden reactions beyond our understanding and control.

"Every time I go out with a boy and come home after midnight my mother is waiting up for me, and she screams at me and calls me a whore," said a fifteen-year-old girl in the course of a counseling session. "If I didn't think better of myself, I'd shack up with anyone I could find, she makes me feel so shabby and so furious with her. Why does she do that?"

It was obvious that the mother was herself greatly confused about sex in general, and in particular about the sexual attitudes and experiences she had had during her own adolescence. What later emerged, in fact, was that the mother had been quite promiscuous for a year or so as a teenager, had felt guilty about her behavior, and had effectively forgotten these experiences completely. When her daughter began to show an interest in dating, the mother, assaulted unconsciously by memories of her own past, twisted and distorted her perceptions of her daughter's behavior, seeing herself instead but unable to acknowledge the very real differences between them, and attacking her daughter as she might have attacked herself.

There is always a highly personal element in determining what will constitute stress for any individual. One person thrives on uncertainty; another is immobilized by it and finds that he can be most comfortable in a way of life in which rules are well defined and goals are clearly spelled out. Divorce or the death of someone in the immediate family will create greater stress for a person who has already been sensitized to loss earlier in life, or who has become excessively dependent on the person he or she loves. Economic reverses will be more of a stress to someone who has invested a great deal of self-esteem in making money and having the things that money can buy. Becoming successful, whether suddenly or after a long period of hard work—achieving fame, wealth, or power, or all three—can, for those who are vulnerable, activate a false sense of personal superiority that can corrupt the very purpose of their lives, lead them to tear down that they have built, and throw into turmoil their relationships with those close to them or those who have accepted their leadership.

The Real Pattern of Psychological Growth

Turning points and periods of transition are more than just episodes of stress. They are important way stations on the road to—for lack of a better phrase—psychological maturity. If one could plot these points on a curve representing psychological growth, the result would not be a straight line upward. It would, instead, be characterized by periodic peaks and valleys, like the tracing of an electrocardiogram. With every new stress and disturbance in the individual's equilibrium, there is a downward movement, which is then followed by the need to restore balance.

This pattern conflicts with what we have been conditioned to expect. Unconsciously, we draw a parallel between physical growth and psychological growth that presumes movement in a single direction; this image derives logically, from childhood, when growth really did mean getting larger. I still can visualize the hall leading from the kitchen to the back door of our house, where the pencil marks on the wall indicated inch by inch how much I had grown each year. Physical growth proceeds in only one direction, upward, until it stops. Psychological growth requires interruptions, a certain amount of pain and confusion before each major advance, and it does not have to stop.

The peaks and valleys that characterize the upward movement of psychological growth force a reconsideration of the highly controversial Freudian postulate of a "death instinct." Freud tells us,

> In the multicellular living organism the libido [life force] meets the death or destructive instinct which holds sway there, and which tries to disintegrate this cellular living being and bring each elemental primary organism into a condition of inorganic stability. . . . To the libido falls the task of making this destructive instinct harmless.

Cruelty—or sadism, as the psychoanalysts termed it—was considered one reflection of this instinct. The will to power was another, and this, if properly channeled, could become the ability to master one's world, one's skill, oneself. There was a biological basis for Freud's theory: If the inevitable end-result of all living matter is death, then there must be a force toward death in every human being even as there is a force for life.

Contemporary psychoanalytic thinking, by and large, rejects this theory. But in doing so it may have overlooked what Freud, having perceived, misinterpreted. Rather than being some kind of propulsion toward the grave, the so-called death instinct may actually be that part of the human personality which is required for the disintegrative or falling-apart phase of the normal response to stress. The greater the stress and the more profound its impact, and the greater the demand for recovery to a higher level, the more disruptive the shock will be to the individual.

There is plenty of evidence in the collective history of mankind to support such a concept. In Christian theology, the admonition to "die in order to be born again" has been taken to mean a promise of life after death. But it can also be interpreted within the framework of each person's own evolution throughout life, so that the process of adaptation to stress, especially at life's turning points, becomes a series of deaths and rebirths on a psychological rather than a physical plane. And it is precisely when people cannot fall apart, or cannot fall apart and recover, that they enter a condition in which most of their energy is spent holding themselves together in one piece, while a crippling spiritual and emotional corrosion goes on underneath.

4
High Blood Pressure and Other Obsolete Responses

One of the most common and socially acceptable ways of reacting to stress is one of the most damaging. It is called psychosomatic illness, and very often reflects a singular lack of psychological adaptability.

Psychosomatic Illness: How Not to Cope

When Bill Alden graduated from high school he was the all-American high school success—first in his class, editor of the school newspaper, captain of the football team. He was reasonably popular with girls, a little self-conscious but no more so than most boys of his age. Seventeen years later, Bill Alden had high blood pressure, not all the time but frequently enough to indicate the need for medications to lower it and prevent the diseases of the heart and blood vessels which would follow, in his forties and fifties, if it could not be stabilized.

What had happened during the intervening years? Bill

didn't smoke. He watched his diet in a reasonable way, avoiding too much cholesterol and salt. He exercised regularly, jogging for half an hour every morning. He was married to a woman with whom he was reasonably compatible. They had two children. His father, who had died of heart disease when Bill was twenty-eight, had left a substantial amount of money, enough to make Bill and his wife financially secure. Had he simply inherited a proclivity for cardiovascular trouble, or was there more to it than that?

"I've never been able to find myself as far as work is concerned," he told me. "When I went to college—a good one, Colgate—I could never really make the grade. I passed. But where I had been a really good student before, I pulled down to a two point seven average, just enough to get by and barely enough to get into law school. There's no doubt in my mind that letters of recommendation made a big difference.

"In the beginning, I couldn't concentrate effectively. In my second year at college, they put me into a special studies group. I felt like a real failure. Any drive I had to do well disappeared. Besides, I didn't have any idea what I wanted to do with myself after college. My father thought I should be a lawyer—a professional, with the security and status that goes with it. So I went to law school, made the decision by default, you could say. He was always on my back, disapproving, telling me what to do and what not to do. I was actually terrified sometimes to talk to him on the phone. He'd ask me how I was doing and I'd have to tell him and there would be a long silence at the other end, and then a lecture about shaping up and working harder. I was working as hard as I could and hating every minute of it.

"After law school, I took the first job offered me, with a small firm in Los Angeles. I was nothing but a glorified office boy. The senior partner had a vicious temper. I stayed there two years, hating every minute of that, too. Then I landed a job, through a friend, with a large company, and I worked in their legal department for five years. I didn't really like it there either. It was monotonous work. When I was passed over for a promotion, I really got angry and quit.

"That's when I started my own practice, here in Carmel. It isn't much of a practice, as law practices go—I made eleven thousand dollars last year. A lot of time is wasted. Just as well, since I really don't have much confidence in myself anyway. I get so anxious sometimes that when I go into court just to file a brief, I think that somehow I'm going to get discovered as a fraud and thrown out of the profession. I get terrified of making a mistake.

"Strangely enough, my wife has a lot of confidence in me. And she doesn't push at all. She often says I should do what I want to do, but I really don't know what that is. I don't know what you can do for me. If it weren't for the suggestion of my doctor, I wouldn't be here. He thinks there's a connection between my blood pressure and what's going on in my head."

Like Bill Alden, most people base their lives on certain premises which are so simple and yet so complex in their radiation throughout the bits and pieces of a lifetime that they often astonish us when we discover what they are. Alden's premises were: "There is something special and unique about me, as an individual, but there isn't anything in my life to confirm that feeling" and "I always have to do what my father wants; he knows better than I do" and "I can't stand controversy; every disagreement with anyone I care about has to be settled quickly, right away." And again, "When anything goes wrong, it must be my fault." These premises did not serve him well in the transition from high school to college—the first time he had ever been away from home. And when, for numerous reasons, he was unable to meet the challenges of the new environment immediately and successfully, he embarked on a pattern of moving from one near-failure to another, motivated by forces he failed to comprehend, each one reinforcing the one which preceded it, but no one of them inducing a sufficient degree of emotional upheaval to force him to come to terms with his situation or himself.

Lacking insight and envisioning no interesting options for himself, Bill Alden translated the growing anger and desperation that he experienced just below the level of consciousness into a physical response which progressed steadily, silently, dangerously, over the years. As if he were reacting to some immediate threat to his life, he called on the systems within his body—his heart and arteries—to ready himself for an onslaught that never really came.

His response was one that is all too common: to activate, inappropriately, an evolutionary residue of survival instincts in an attempt to cope with complex, psychological, twentieth-century stress as if it were some imminent physical danger. As a way of responding to stress, the heart and the blood vessels provide a far more primitive method of maintaining or restoring our equilibrium—and safety—

in the face of sudden shocks or changes imposed by a hostile environment. They are by no means completely obsolete. To stay alive in a physical crisis—such as having a tire suddenly blow out when you are driving along a freeway—demands an immediate reaction, a tightening of the muscles, a racing of the heart, an elevation in blood pressure, a sharpening of alertness, all of which permit you, in a fraction of a second, to keep the automobile in control long enough to prevent it from careening off the road or into someone else's car. Once you are safe, the biological changes reverse themselves as you settle down, physically and emotionally.

Bill Alden was reacting to a series of complex psychological and environmental stresses, existing and reinforcing themselves over a period of years, as if he were reacting to a sudden and unexpected shock to his physical integrity. In this sense, his response can only be seen as obsolete and inappropriate—at best ineffective, at worst self-destructive. Paradoxically, however, it is the most socially acceptable response in keeping with the values of today's society, in which most people would find it more bearable, less embarrassing, and less threatening to react to stress with a physical disturbance than with a psychological one.

As an assistant marketing manager for a large retail chain put it: "Can you imagine what my boss's reaction would be if I went to him and said, 'I feel like I'm falling apart; I'm probably depressed; my doctor wants me to take a few weeks off and get some psychotherapy'? He'd think I was crazy. Sure, he'd probably be understanding, tell me to go ahead, but I'm positive he'd already be thinking about whom he could find to replace me and what the hell he'd do with me when I came back to work. On the other hand, if I went in and said, 'I've got these pains in my chest; my doctor is worried about my heart and wants to have me take a few weeks off,' I know I'd get his full support."

Values such as these do not always serve us well, even when they purport to serve the interests of progress. As more and more women assume the kind of rights and responsibilities in the world of business that men have, they have begun, not surprisingly, to show the same tendency to revert to physical reactions as a response to psychological and social pressures. The Americanization of Japan, with the concomitant liberation of Japanese women from domestic isolation, has brought in its wake a fourfold increase in the incidence of coronary heart disease among women in that country.

Traditionally, women have been freer than men to respond to upsetting events with emotional reactions. In our culture in particular, a man is expected and expects himself to weather any distressing event coolly, calmly, unemotionally. Small wonder, then, that his vulnerability to heart disease is so much greater than that of women. When stresses occur, the human being must respond, somehow, in self-protection. If emotional responses are not "permitted," physical responses will take their place.

When I was still a medical student, I was fortunate in having as professor of neurology and medicine one of the pioneers in psychosomatic medicine, Harold G. Wolf. We now take for granted so much that was then in an embryonic stage that we tend to forget how original the studies of Dr. Wolf and his colleagues were. These researchers were especially interested in the connection between psychological stress and physical health. In particular, they attempted to demonstrate how certain personality traits and strong emotional conflicts were causally related to such conditions as migraine headache and gastrointestinal disturbance.

Among Dr. Wolf's better-known cases was that of a patient named Tom, who, because of a gunshot wound years before, had a fistula that permitted the lining of his stomach to be exposed for study. When upset, and in particular when angry, Tom would reveal a red and engorged stomach and would secrete large amounts of gastric acid. Patients with ulcers of the stomach or the small intestine, these doctors suggested, may possess a unique vulnerability to the destruction of mucosal tissue and hence be extremely susceptible to the biological effects of disturbing emotions, particularly those which are unrecognized and unresolved, such as pent-up rage.

In those days, researchers in psychosomatic medicine went so far as to attempt to define the kind of person who was most likely to develop a particular symptom pattern. The person likely to develop chronic constipation, for example, was envisioned as a constricted, stubborn sort of individual. By contrast, the one who readily developed diarrhea or forms of colitis was described as being more passive, less able to persevere in reaching goals, more likely to give up in a hurry. Subsequent study has shown that some of these early concepts were unduly simplistic and that such specificity was not truly tenable. Nevertheless, this trend has continued—to such a degree, in fact, that the book by Drs. Meyer Friedman and Ray Rosenman in which they try to show a strong correlation between the occurrence of heart attacks and the ambitious, hard-driving, achievement-oriented, perfectionist, time-constricted executive—the so-called Type A personality—was called "must" reading by a former president of the American College of Cardiology.

That a person can respond to psychological stress with respiratory disorders, heart disease, migraine headaches, or ulcers is now beyond dispute. But in the attempt to narrow the connection between the mind and the body to particular traits and conflicts, most psychosomatic formulations have overlooked or at least failed to emphasize the common denominator. People who react to situations of conflict by triggering a physical illness such as a heart attack invariably lack an inner emotional life that is in any way relevant to what they are experiencing.

As their Type A candidate for a heart attack, Drs. Friedman and Rosenman described an individual who is

> *aggressively* involved in a *chronic, incessant* struggle to achieve more and more in less and less time and if required to do so, against the opposing efforts of other things or other persons. . . . The fundamental sickness of the Type A subject consists of his peculiar failure to perceive, or perhaps worse, to accept the simple fact that a man's time can be exhausted by his activities. . . . He substitutes repetitive urgency for creative energy. . . . Because of his obsession with numbers and because so many of the world's activities are expressed in currency units . . . the Type A subject more often than not appears to be absorbed in money. . . . Most Type A subjects possess so much aggressive drive that it frequently evolves into a free-floating hostility [even if] they keep such feelings and impulses under deep cover.

The Lack of Insight

Basically, the kind of person they are describing has little or no insight, either into himself as a person or into the subtle as well as the more striking aspects of other people's psychological makeup. His self-esteem must be considered extremely brittle, regardless of the self-confidence which the authors describe, inasmuch as he has never learned to separate his personal identity from that which stems from his accomplishments. If he is hostile, he has certainly never learned how to relinquish angry or aggressive feelings and probably does not understand the art of reconciliation or forgiveness. He is involved in denying the more emotional and intuitive components of his personality. He will limit his options so rigidly that if and when life confronts him with a series of circumstances which threaten to overwhelm him, he must necessarily fall back on physical impairment and sometimes even death rather than allow himself the freedom to become depressed.

Hospitals are filled with patients whose style of living and lack of insight are major reasons for their heart attacks, bleeding ulcers, and migraine headaches. But I was particularly struck by the connection between psychosomatic illness and lack of awareness when, as a resident physician, I encountered its exact opposite—the person who quite readily attributed his physical distress to emotional problems, only to be found suffering from a serious physical illness. I was asked to see a fifty-year-old man who had been admitted to the psychiatric division of the hospital because his many special complaints had not yielded to outpatient psychotherapy stretching over nearly a year's time. When I

walked into his room to carry out the initial admission examination, he was sitting up in bed, protesting that he
should get up and get going even though he felt weak and
confused. "I can't give into this—I know that! My head
hurts terribly. But I know it's all due to conflict, tensions I
haven't been able to resolve."

My suspicion was instinctively aroused by his insistence
on the psychological basis of his problems, especially since
I had already learned how little insight those people
usually have who react to stress with physical symptoms
rather than emotional ones. I arranged for him to have a
complete medical and laboratory investigation. The diagnosis was chronic uremic poisoning resulting from long-
standing kidney damage.

It is important to make a clear distinction between physical changes that are natural components of an emotional
response—when you are afraid, your pulse rate will
usually rise, regardless of the stimulus—and those that are
actually a substitute for an emotional reaction, such as an
attack of intestinal pain and episodes of diarrhea instead of
the experience of fear. It is also important to consider
another set of conditions in which physical changes take
the place of psychological ones; here, though the pain and
crippling effects may be very real to the person experiencing them, the physician can demonstrate absolutely no
medical basis for them, and no diagnosis can be made, either by physical examination or laboratory testing. These
are called dissociative reactions. The feelings are shut off,
and their place is taken by physical symptoms. People experiencing a dissociative state are as lacking in insight as
those who have psychosomatic illnesses, although they

may often demonstrate considerable cleverness in the manner in which they form their symptoms and use them to adapt to stressful circumstances.

Dave Mitchell was forty-three years old, a successful advertising executive. He had never had any physical diseases except measles and chicken pox. Nor had he ever had any changes in his moods or emotional life that he considered worthy of attention.

"I've never been depressed," he declared. "I've always been in good spirits, rolling with the punches. No, I don't have a temper, but then I take a philosophical attitude toward most things. What I'm going through now scares the hell out of me.

"I get this terrific pressure in my chest sometimes. At other times I get dizzy, light-headed, as if I might fall over in a faint. I've been to my doctor a dozen times in the last three months alone, and he can't find a thing wrong with me. I even keep a blood-pressure cuff at home. My wife's a nurse. She's taken it a number of times when these attacks come on, and there's no change. I used to enjoy playing tennis and skiing. For the past year I haven't done either. Any kind of physical exertion, especially if it's competitive, sets it off. I've been trying to connect it with upsetting situations—and believe me I have plenty of them—but there's no predictable pattern. I'm convinced that there's something wrong with me physically, but why can't anyone find out what? My life is literally falling apart. I don't want to go anywhere most of the time. My wife has taken to doing her own thing and I can understand why. Who wants to sit around the house all weekend listening to me complain?"

One year before he sought psychiatric help, Dave Mitchell's mother had died after a terminal illness, cancer, that lasted two years. "I didn't cry, not when she died, not at the funeral. I just didn't think about her at all. She was a simple woman. I can't recall any problems with her. In fact, I don't have any memories of her at all. Should I?" There was a curious naïveté about the way in which he spoke about himself and his life. "When my wife got angry at me for canceling out on that dinner party last week, at the last minute, because I was afraid I might not feel well, I didn't feel a thing, didn't react to her anger at all. Should I have felt something?"

Dave Mitchell was demonstrating what might be called a classic dissociative reaction. Automatically, without conscious intent, he was blocking out any and all memories of his mother—and with these, innumerable recollections of his childhood and adolescence, some of which related to her and many of which did not—in his own personal effort to deal with the enormous, unrecognized grief triggered by her death and lingering without resolution.

The net effect of his so-called physical disability was to limit his activities, isolate him from his wife, cause him to suffer and to fear some kind of sudden, fatal illness—all of which are reactions quite similar to those associated with depression. But he did not feel depressed. "If I could feel better physically," he maintained, "I'd be fine."

In the course of psychotherapy—forty or so visits over a period of six months—he was finally able to remember specific events out of the past, pleasant and unpleasant, which had a bearing on the quality of the relationship he had had with his mother. Sometimes the details would appear indirectly, through a dream. Sometimes they would come in response to a question from his psychiatrist. And as these recollections emerged, complete with the details and feelings originally attached to the events, his physical symptoms gradually disappeared.

The release of memories of the past from the bond of dissociation was the fundamental step in early psychoanalysis as developed by Freud and his associates. By the mid-1940s this type of cure was big box office for Hollywood— *The Snake Pit, Spellbound,* and *The Three Faces of Eve*—so much so that the popular image of what happens in psychotherapy revolved around such a series of liberating moments. Thousands of patients were consequently disappointed when they improved substantially without ever having experienced the dramatic breakthrough of re-calling some profoundly disturbing event in early childhood that could account for their problems.

Dissociative reactions have become less and less common during the past half century as people have become more knowledgeable and more sophisticated in their methods of creating neurotic modes of behavior. Rarely, except among more primitive peoples and less educated groups within the general population, does one see the paralyzed arm, the complete state of blindness, the superficial pain that follows no known nerve-distribution pattern and shifts even as the needle of the neurologist passes over the skin. We have become much too clever to be caught attempting to win attention or sympathy, manipulate or punish ourselves, with methods so easily detected by an astute clinician, or even, nowadays, by a child in front of the television set watching a rerun of Ingrid Bergman trying to help Gregory Peck remember whether "Rome" means Rome, Italy, or Rome, New York.

The individual who reacts to stress by substituting a physical response for a psychological one pays a high price indeed for failing to cultivate insight and come to terms with the real issues. Meanwhile, as the dissociative type of response becomes rarer and rarer, we have discovered new ways to hide those key issues from ourselves, and thereby postpone inevitable confrontations, by translating our problems, again without insight, into patterns of behavior that attempt to solve our inner distress by tampering with things outside of us.

The Great Escape

There is nothing new about running away from problems. Nor is it always the wrong reaction. In fact, there are times when distancing oneself, temporarily or permanently, from a troublesome situation is clearly the best course to take. However, in an era when a trip from New York to California is no more complicated to arrange than dialing a telephone number and presenting a credit card, the opportunities for fleeing from stress are multiplied geometrically. Running away, of course, is only one of the more obvious methods (alcohol being another) of avoiding insight and the need to come to terms with ourselves.

The comment that we have become perpetual adolescents has some basis, though such an observation is not entirely fair to the adolescent. Rather then resolving inner emotional conflicts by changing ourselves, we have developed a tendency to translate these problems into action. The middle-aged executive, unable to acknowledge that he is distressed by the coming of age, sexually and otherwise, of his daughters and by the fact that he may have reached the highest rung on the corporate ladder he has so assiduously climbed, may find a year or two of fragile rejuvenation with his secretary. This kind of behavior pattern is called adolescent because the teenage years are marked by a groping for insight on the part of the youngster who lacks the perspective, or what should be the perspective, of the adult. Adolescents are far more likely than adults to act on impulses in an erratic and seemingly unpredictable manner, especially when under stress. The solution to an unhappy school situation is to quit. The resolution of a love relationship that has developed problems is to break it off. The response to feeling misunderstood by the family is to become uncommunicative for several days at a time.

Teenagers are particularly susceptible to the pressure placed on them by friends to behave in ways that are condoned or encouraged by the group, whether or not these standards are naïve and in serious conflict with the expectations of parents and teachers. The vulnerability of adolescents is increased by differences among families with regard to what is and what is not acceptable behavior. These differences, in turn, are accentuated by the lack of strong, universally shared ethical attitudes within the culture as a whole. Some parents may show no interest in their children's education, while others may repeatedly apply pressure for higher and higher levels of achievement. In one home, minor infractions may be dealt with immediately and severely, while in another rules governing the conduct of family members may be poorly defined and rarely, if ever, enforced.

When parents meet at a parent-teacher conference, the

conversations reveal the conflict in expectations between school and home, but mostly those between one home and another. "I have to give my children some freedom; how else will they learn to be responsible?" one mother will ask, only to have another declare, "I care about the kind of youngsters my kids associate with. I think I should have a lot to say about the places they go and what they do."

The dilemma faced by adolescents is no longer unique to them. They are not the only ones subject to peer pressure, left to create their own set of values without sufficient knowledge or experience. They are not alone in building expectations and ambitions which are less rooted in reality than in the subjective world of their own feelings or, especially, in the poorly understood recesses of the unconscious. With alarming acceleration, adults of every age are finding themselves confused with regard to what they consider acceptable and unacceptable behavior. Urged on by promises of something better somewhere, somehow, they press for the immediate resolution of difficulties which by their very nature cannot be resolved at once, rejecting situations that seem unsatisfactory—relationships, jobs, marriages—instead of reappraising either themselves or the situation in an attempt to arrive at a better level of life within the framework of what already exists.

From a psychiatrist's vantage point, this cultural shift shows up as a major alteration in the way in which emotional problems manifest themselves. Nowadays people are more apt to attribute inner distress to difficult life situations than to anything within themselves. Most people are unaware that such situations—the break-up of a marriage, for example—often *result* from the failure to come to terms with a conflict at some earlier point. Ten years ago it was common for people to consult a psychiatrist because they had identified within themselves a change in their ability to function—fears, problems in concentrating, loss of sexual drive—for which they felt the need of some kind of therapy. Distress is still frequently the force that motivates an individual to come to a psychiatrist, but that distress is now more commonly seen as a situation, as some kind of concrete obstacle that only needs to be resolved or removed for everything to run smoothly again.

At the urging of a good friend, Edward King, age thirty-five, arrived at the office of a psychiatrist to discuss his confusion about an extramarital affair he had been having for several months with a girl who worked in his office. He had outlined rather clearly in his mind what he felt was a difficult situation; it was only the details and finer points within the general outline that he felt needed further clarification. "We want to get married," he concluded with an air of urgency. "I just don't know how to settle this with my wife without hurting her."

King had been married for twelve years. He had three small children, and on his income as a sales representative for a tool company he could just manage to keep his financial affairs in order. He described his marriage as "basically all right." In fact, his wife had suggested that he live with the girl to get it out of his system. "But I can't do that. It has to be settled one way or the other, and right now I don't see any choice but to get a divorce and marry Janet."

"Every other person we know has been or is going through a divorce," his wife, Emily, told the psychiatrist in a separate session. "But I never thought it could happen to us. I've been happy all these years. I really love Ed. Whatever problems we have, and obviously we've had our share, we have a lot in common. We like the same things, we like the same people. Our sex life has been good. I don't think he's himself, but, frankly, I don't know what to do about it."

"I've never had a sexual experience like this one, Doctor," Ed said. "And I can't get Janet out of my mind. There was a special kind of chemistry between us from the first minute we met. She feels the same way. It's far more than sex. Incidentally, since our last visit I've been to a lawyer, just to find out what might be involved."

Edward King was hardly the first person to leave his wife for another woman, or to be tempted to do so. Yet in contrast to many dissolving marriages, this one revealed no serious problems within it. Ed and Emily had always been able to communicate well with each other. Until the last few months, it had never occurred to him that he might make a move to end his marriage for any reason whatsoever. Now he was caught up in a "trade-in," exchanging the old model for what seemed to him, on the surface at least, to be a new and better one. Beneath the surface, however, was an extreme vulnerability to his own need to have what he wanted when he wanted it, as well as a tendency to be sullenly obstinate when blocked in his desires. Perhaps even more significant was Ed's lack of a well-defined code of behavior to follow in the face of a crisis that set him up for the control exerted from within his own unconscious.

What was the nature of this unconscious control? It was a model of the relationship his parents had had, which, as such models are inclined to do, was pressuring him to repeat his parents' mistakes and fall into the same patterns that had trapped them. His mother had been a quiet, passive woman, irritatingly indecisive and given to submerging her feelings of hurt or anger in alcohol. Ed's father, treating her with contempt, shouted, criticized, and flaunted his affairs with other women. The behavior of each reinforced that of the other, setting up a vicious circle with little possibility of improvement or resolution.

In another period, Ed might have been influenced by social restrictions to come to terms with his own inner conflicts—something he was capable of doing because he possessed a capacity for insight that his father had evidently lacked or had not been motivated to develop. The conflict between the model of his parents' marriage and the reality of his own marriage might have manifested itself in "symptoms"—anxiety, or a disturbance in his ability to work and concentrate. Instead, he translated his conflicts into behavior, became "astonishingly" involved with Janet, and was ready to end his otherwise good marriage in a matter of a few weeks.

The Risks in Greater Freedom

The relaxing of once commonly accepted standards of behavior provides greater personal freedom, affording many people a unique opportunity to resolve destructive life situations which, in another age, might have crippled them for the rest of their lives. Until recent years, for example, a person who had been through a divorce often lived to some degree in social disgrace. Both men and women in this situation usually regarded themselves as failures. Old friends frequently avoided or directly ostracized them, partly as a kind of moral condemnation, partly because of fear of a potential influence, like a contagious virus, on their own seemingly well-balanced lives. A divorced man was certainly not considered to be a good candidate for a position of responsibility in business, government, or a profession. A divorced woman often led a lonely existence and was expected to pay a high price sexually for the least bit of companionship.

I can recall, in my early days as a resident in psychiatry, being taught that any marriage was to be considered relatively sacrosanct, and that separation and divorce were to be considered only if the patient insisted or if the situation reached such an extreme that it represented a clear, indisputable threat to the patient's future health. In spite of the popular misconception that to see a psychiatrist was inviting the breakup of one's marriage, psychiatrists were frequently engaged in a struggle to strengthen the personality of the patient to a sufficient degree that he or she could live within the framework of a highly demoralizing home environment.

Now a more liberal attitude about the termination of the marriage contract has evolved—even the Catholic Church, once adamant on the permanence of marriage, has extensively revised the grounds on which it will grant annulments. Thousands of people are able to give themselves a second chance by removing themselves from a relationship that has been destructive, sometimes from its very inception.

What is true of marriage is true in other areas of social expectations as well. A banker can desert his profession, if he chooses, and become an organic-food grower. A youngster who would formerly have been expected to struggle on and finish a college education for which he was not suited can drop out and become a highly skilled craftsman. A woman can adopt a child without marrying; so can a man. None of these options involves undue social censure. We have more opportunities to settle real problems and rid ourselves of undesirable handicaps that may have been acquired through inexperience, naïveté, poor judgment, or unfortunate circumstances. But with such progress, a new kind of problem has arisen: the tendency to avoid emotional distress and postpone the resolution of conflicts by means of poorly thought-through changes in environment and behavior.

Sally Blanton was eighteen when she went to the University of California to become an English major and someday, she hoped, a writer. A quiet and sensitive girl, she was an only child and had never been away from home before. She had demonstrated a bright and energetic mind early on in her school, and her parents, neither of whom had finished high school, were proud of her. The three of them had been quite close, traveling together in the summers, going to church on Sundays; when Sally left home, her mother especially felt the emptiness of the house without her.

Sally became somewhat homesick during the first weeks

at college but tried to shut out these feelings and lose herself in her work. Halfway through the first semester she met Harold, a senior. After a few pleasant dates, somewhat reluctantly, and partly out of curiosity and a feeling that she might be one of the few inexperienced girls in her dormitory, she had her first complete sexual experience. "I felt a little guilty," she said, "but I got over that in a hurry. It was a hang-up."

After Harold there was Jim, and after Jim there was Arnie, and after Arnie she decided not to go home for the summer between the first and second year of college and instead went to work in San Francisco as a waitress. Then she decided, having become restless and bored with her studies, to take a year off and "find herself." She lived with Don for six months. "I really loved him, and when he walked out on me, I thought I'd kill myself. But I didn't. It never occurred to me that something might be driving me on to find one boy after another, picking guys who ended up treating me badly. I thought that what I needed was a real change of pace. So I went to live in this commune. I still thought a lot about suicide, but then I decided I'd better eliminate those thoughts and pull myself out of that situation and go back to school. So I came here, last fall. I've been going to classes and working hard. But I can't concentrate, I can't sleep without pills, I feel wretched most of the time."

The contemporary scene is full of opportunities for Sallys of any age to run away from hurting, for a while, in pursuit of a solution to an ill-defined uneasiness which they mistakenly attribute solely to what they are doing and whom they are with at the moment rather than to what is going on within themselves. Several years ago the *Wall Street Journal* published an article entitled, "Why Children of Executives Run Away From Home" and was deluged with requests for reprints from distraught parents. When the solution to a difficult personal relationship or a problem in one's education or career is seen as no more complicated than the problem of getting away from one place to another, this tendency to translate emotional conflicts into impulsive behavior is reinforced by the widespread vulnerability to the power of suggestion.

The Power of Suggestion

Suggestibility is a universal human trait. It varies in intensity from one person to another. It is the basis of hypnosis, during which the range of one's concentration is progressively narrowed until consciousness is fixed so that subconscious recollections can emerge or instructions for some seemingly illogical behavior, such as suddenly whistling a tune on the count of three, will be followed after one awakens. Suggestibility was the basis for the epidemic of suicides among young men that followed the publication of Goethe's novel *The Sorrows of Young Werther* and for the mass hysteria among young women at the time of the Salem witch trials.

Experiments have definitely shown that when one's anxiety level is raised—as during a period of extreme stress or in anticipation of an event which one expects to be painful—the threshold for suggestibility is lowered and one becomes much more vulnerable to external influences and direction. Ambiguous messages, or messages that are implied and not made clear, provoke anxiety and heighten suggestibility. And when there are no well-defined values, the anxiety level and the susceptibility to suggestion usually rise sharply, urging people on to action which will rapidly free them from the disagreeable and give them a maximum degree of immediate pleasure. The net result of this popular form of handling stress is that people impulsively act out their inner conflicts with only the dimmest grasp of their motivations.

The balance that should exist between thought and action has been so shifted that we tend to consider the sources of unhappiness and the avenues of self-fulfillment as largely, if not exclusively, external. If we can change our circumstances, we can solve our problems. When therapists or proponents of meditation tell us to look inward for answers, this all too often promotes the opposite mistake—we are encouraged not to take any action, even when action of some sort is clearly necessary.

Moreover, we are misled into believing that we must make a choice between inner change and altering our environment to suit our apparent needs when, in fact, such a choice has no validity at all. It is not a case of one or the other. Rather, we should try to be guided by greater self-knowledge and a more accurate appraisal of reality, and to free ourselves from any destructive residue of the past which might keep us from choosing the new directions that are truly best for our future.

One of the most serious deterrents to doing what would otherwise seem obviously sensible is the frightening prospect of falling apart, or allowing our world to fall apart, as we move through these stages of the creative process toward change. But only when we can master the ability to do exactly this can we discover, afterward, a new kind of personal coherence.

6
The Art
of Falling Apart

The best response to psychological stress is a psychological response; it not only signals that there is a need for change in ourselves and in our environment, but it is a necessary step toward insight and finding appropriate solutions.

Consider, by analogy, the decided advantage of the pain experienced with appendicitis. If your abdomen hurts from the inflammation of the appendix, you will rush immediately to a doctor to find out what's wrong. If you did not feel the sharp, stabbing pains in the right lower belly, you would ignore the other, milder signs of the condition until the appendix ruptured and the condition became dangerous.

Psychological pain serves similar ends. Episodes of anxiety, outbursts of anger, and periods of depression are all warning signs. They motivate one to rethink situations and resolve them. They are, moreover, inherently restorative. Crying or losing one's temper—about the right issues and at the right time—relieves inner tension.

Such emotions and moods indicate a shift in balance. They necessarily disrupt the smooth flow of things. They can be quite uncomfortable and are likely to interfere with one's ability to concentrate, stay in control, maintain some semblance of equanimity. Yet the very harmony they disrupt may be superficial and basically detrimental.

Consider the failure to recognize and deal with conflict. A forty-two-year-old married woman, a patient of mine, had always found it extremely difficult to react emotionally to provocations by her husband, or by anyone else for that matter, burying her feelings in order to preserve stability in her relationships. "I got on well with everyone," she observed, when she might have said, more accurately, "I felt I couldn't afford to let things get stirred up, even if the price I paid for this was my own self-respect."

Over the years, the closeness that she had earlier had with her husband gradually eroded. It was replaced by boredom, a painful feeling that she also preferred to ignore. The balance she had maintained was rudely shattered when she discovered that her husband was involved in an affair with a mutual friend.

No human relationship is static. It changes, as people change and circumstances change. Intimacy itself periodically touches nerve endings—areas of dispute which, if numbed, can fester beneath the surface to undermine the relationship. Conflict, even when it leads to anger, if handled creatively and with consideration, may actually clear the air and encourage an imaginative resolution of the problem that provoked it.

Unfortunately, many people do not even possess the vocabulary to describe what they are experiencing emotionally, much less to know how to interpret their feelings correctly and be guided by them. Some years ago I was responsible for teaching introductory human behavior to first-year medical students at Cornell. Instead of focusing immediately on the theories of behavior as such, I directed the program toward an examination of the kinds of problems and experiences that are common to men and women in their early twenties, especially to those who had chosen medicine as a career. It seemed to me that plunging at once into Freud's libidinal theory would be quite irrelevant to students who were, for the first time in their lives, confronted with the awesome task of learning the intricacies of the human body in the anatomy laboratory and of becoming involved in a kind of hypochondriacal dissection of themselves as well. And the enormous pressure on their time, the demands of competition and of study, and the anticipation of the responsibilities they would shortly be assuming with patients could not be ignored.

My unorthodox approach had several remarkable results. To begin with, most of the students denied that any of these pressures made them uncomfortable—until they began to talk about what the pressures were and to realize their feelings about them. One spoke of resenting the competition; another of being unable to fall asleep at night, staying up to study until three or four in the morning and feeling exhausted the next day; another of his girl friend breaking off with him because they didn't have enough time together. They were genuinely surprised to realize that others had feelings similar to their own and just as much trouble finding the words to describe them.

At one session I asked, "How many know what loneliness is?" There were ninety students present. Only about a dozen put up their hands. A few seconds later, about ten more did so. I asked one of them to describe what it was like to be lonely. "It's something more than just being by yourself," he said. "It hurts a lot. There's a longing in it, for someone, and a sense of emptiness." I asked again how many had experienced loneliness. Fifty more hands went up.

Then I asked how many had ever been depressed. No hands were raised. I became more specific. How many had gone through periods of feeling very real sadness? How many had grieved after someone in the family had died? How many knew the anguish of a broken love relationship? How many were plagued at times with self-doubt and lowered self-confidence? With each new question, more and more hands went up. Gradually my message became clear: Depression is a normal response to certain kinds of stresses, especially those that involve the loss of someone or something valued or of one's own self-esteem.

To respond appropriately to psychological stress, one must learn some set of terms to describe, even if only to oneself, what one is experiencing. This is the first step toward insight. It enables one to recognize the source of the trouble and to begin considering solutions.

Depression Is a Normal Response to Stress

Depression of mood is perhaps the most characteristic signal that precedes and accompanies significant personal change. While we are all familiar with the fact that grief will follow the death of someone close to us, we are less familiar with the fact that grief—which is a form of depression—will accompany any major life change. Such a change, whether it is getting married, reaching fifty, getting divorced, failing in business, or retiring, is inevitably associated with loss—loss of freedom, loss of youth, loss of financial security. We are even less aware that a significant change in the way we look at things, including ourselves, means that we have let go of previously important premises and so will experience some degree of depression.

The idea that falling apart—being temporarily immobilized by depression, for example—can serve any constructive purpose is alien to our way of thinking. The person who always remains calm under pressure is held in high regard. Fear is often considered a sign of weakness. To collapse in the face of stressful conditions is not only seen as weak but frequently and mistakenly raises the specter of mental illness or an irreversible drift toward chronic instability.

The facts are quite the opposite. Most people who become depressed recover. Most creative, accomplished people have reported periods of depression just before a new surge of personal growth and achievement.

Why, then, is there such reluctance to fall apart when this is clearly called for? Beyond the embarrassment (which is inappropriate), beyond the natural abhorrence of helplessness (which is understandable), beyond the sense of vulnerability to those around us (which is a result of living in a blatantly competitive society), our unwillingness to fall apart in preparation for a new and better way of coping is closely linked to age-old myths that surround what is called "mental illness."

Sometimes the disintegrative stage in the creative response to stress can be quite dramatic. In the course of personal change, the greater the resistance—the tougher the fiber of the personality or the more tightly glued together the system of interpersonal relationships—the more intense is the inner disruption that may be exacted to produce a state of renewal. A series of severe stresses can set off such a strong reaction that the emotional state may appear indistinguishable from those conditions which, because of complex biological origins, are viewed as mental illness.

Richard Bragen was thirty-eight when his father died. Two months later his sixteen-year old daughter announced that she was pregnant. His marriage, which had survived rather uneventfully for nearly eighteen years, collapsed two months after that; his wife, disturbed by the problems they shared, impulsively but firmly decided to solve her own conflicts by getting a divorce.

Richard had been more or less holding himself together, but when he received a letter from his wife's attorney informing him of her intent and when his pleading with her to try again accomplished nothing, he rapidly began to fall apart. He considered suicide but rejected it outright because of the children. He went for ten days with little more than two or three hours of sleep a night. His performance at work deteriorated completely. When his wife called the family physician to the house, Richard was sitting alone on the edge of his bed, sobbing.

He spent six weeks in a psychiatric hospital. There he

was treated with medications to quiet his pain and given a chance to release his anguish and talk about his future with a doctor. He gradually regained his composure. He returned to work and began the complicated process of re-structuring his life. He found a place to live. He began to search for new friendships, since many of those he had had previously were interwoven with his marriage and so were no longer available to him. He was reassured by the continued love and respect of his children, and as the pain gradually eased, he found himself living in a different kind of world, where he was even at times exhilarated: "Not only have I been able to find new interests and pick up some of those I had let slide over the years, but getting through this has definitely given me a new kind of strength."

The common assumption would be that Richard Bragen had suffered some kind of mental illness. In truth, he had not. His reaction to the devastating impact of a series of stresses, compressed into a brief period of time, was in fact quite appropriate. Moreover, the stresses forced a change in him that was essential if he was to construct a new life with the least possible interference from the residue of the past.

The majority of people who have consulted me over the years, regardless of how much they have been suffering or how much they have been incapacitated at any particular moment, seem healthier mentally than many others I have encountered outside the consulting room. The latter, lack-ing insight, unmotivated to improve, blaming their prob-lems on people around them, rarely if ever seek professional help. Working things out, to them, always depends on someone else's changing.

In other words, you cannot define mental illness by dividing people into those who seek help and those who do not. Nor can you define it by the ability a person has to control feelings at all times and to stay in one piece no matter how intense the pressure.

There seems to be a very fine line indeed that separates an acceptable type and degree of emotional distress from a condition that could be called an illness. So fine, in fact, is the distinction that in recent years such psychiatrists as R. D. Laing and Thomas Szasz have declared that there is no such thing as mental illness. Rather, they state, patients who have been viewed as mentally ill are responding to adverse personal and social circumstances that breed "sickness," and their conditions should be viewed instead as a normal reaction to a very mixed-up society. Mental illness, they propose, is actually in the eye of the beholder.

There is much to be said for this position. As psychological thinking broke out of the constraints of Freudian psychoanalytic theory and began to consider seriously the role that environmental forces play in the formation of unhealthy patterns of thought and behavior, it rapidly became apparent that there were indeed environments which would force a person into a position of sickness as an expected, if not a required, form of adaptation. In many instances, a so-called patient was shown to have been subjected to the insensitivities and cruelties of others who, usually unwittingly, handled their own problems by finding scapegoats from whom they could exact punishment.

As a systems approach to human interaction has evolved, it has become easier to see how the relationships that exist among members of a group, whether it is a family or an organization, determines to a large extent the behavior of each member of the group. Someone may be declared "unstable," and his continued participation in that role may become an essential part of machinery for the functioning of the entire system. By the same token, recovery in a patient often leads to major changes in the nature of the group relationships and in the character of the group itself, even to the point where, like a series of dominoes, other family members may collapse into a variety of neurotic conditions. The pattern of control is broken. The unwritten insistence on undue dependency is shattered. And those who derived strength from the original premises are suddenly confronted with the need to find new ones.

However, an important criticism of the Laingian position can also be made. There is a very real difference between falling apart, however dramatically, in the face of stress, in the interests of personal growth and readjustment or as part of a creative experience, and being "ill." This difference rests on two factors: the individual's capacity to tolerate and actually benefit from a certain amount of stress, and his or her ability to recover from the disorganizing impact of a situation, such as a significant failure, that demands falling apart.

Under ordinary circumstances, most of us can limit the extent to which stress affects us. It is one thing to lie in bed, robbed of the spirit of life, thinking about wanting to die, but still keeping enough perspective to know that this mood will pass; it is quite another to balance precariously on the edge of a bridge, ready to jump. There is a real difference between being unable to go to work for a few weeks because you cannot concentrate well enough to make intelligent decisions and don't care about those decisions anyway, and starting to hear strange voices that accuse you of being a vicious, despicable person disliked by everyone you work with.

Most of us possess psychological and biological brakes that ordinarily limit how upset we get. An equally critical factor for coping, however, is our ability to pull ourselves together afterward—to reintegrate—and this is a faculty that many people have never really put to the test. It is the final stage in the creative process. Things begin to fall into place. A new structure is being formed. And the ultimate difference between normal reactions to change and those more severe, tenacious conditions that are sometimes regarded as illness will most likely be found to be primarily a function of one's capacity to recover.

This ability to recover requires us to be skilled in those processes necessary to change attitudes and values, notably the exercise of creativity. Paradoxically, even among people who suffer definite mental and behavioral changes that actually represent forms of illness—the schizophrenias, for example—the presence of creative personality traits enables the therapist to predict a much higher rate of improvement. However, even when recovery is impeded, it is still presumptuous to assume a diagnosis of mental illness, for some people live in environments that are indeed damaging and unyielding and from which they have not yet discovered an exit.

Biological Determinants

Just where, then, does the distinction lie? The evidence that exists points strongly to the probability that the difference between normal stress reactions and illness rests in one's biological makeup. There are physiological obstacles to recovery. For certain forms of mental and behavioral problems—those which for purposes of diagnosis and treatment are referred to as the schizophrenias or the manic-depressive syndrome—there is growing support for the belief that genetic factors contribute to the problem. This means that such patients are born with certain biological deficits which make it hard, and at times impossible, for them to achieve a healthy response to stress.

Every person operates simultaneously as a psychological and a biological unit—for every thought and feeling there is a chemical or physiological change in the nervous system. Consequently, the ability to fall apart and reorganize oneself again in a reasonable period of time requires that these biological pathways be operating efficiently. When there are flaws in them, such as a predisposition to throw out excessive amounts of steroid hormones or to excrete too much calcium from the body, the individual lacks the necessary physical components to adjust to change. The facts that a drug such as chlorpromazine will interrupt the delusions and voices that some psychiatric patients believe and hear, and that another drug such as imipramine will restore normal spirits to someone who had been trapped for years in chronic depression, argue strongly for the presence of such important physiological correlates to the response to stress.

As problematic as mental and emotional disturbances may be, regardless of cause, they represent from an evolutionary point of view a higher level of adaptation than the more socially acceptable psychosomatic illnesses or culturally encouraged forms of "acting out." The psychiatric patient is responding psychologically to psychological stress, irrespective of the degree of his handicap. And this response is a more human and appropriate route than the alternatives, for it carries with it the seeds of its own resolution. Emotionally disturbed persons are not only more likely to look into themselves for answers and to re-examine their relationships in order to consider necessary changes, but their suffering in itself propels them toward new awareness and ultimately to choices based on these new insights.

In my experience as a physician, it is extremely difficult to convince those whose reactions to stress are largely physical that headaches, pains in the chest or back, or dizzy spells are connected with their marriage, conditions at work, or personal values. It is equally difficult to persuade those who have found temporary respite in the exploitation of others, who have repeatedly shown poor judgment in the formation of relationships or in financial decisions, or who have used alcohol as a way to cope with distress, to look at themselves and their situation and come to terms with them. By contrast, the person who is depressed and knows it is often eager to make changes which may have been long overdue and to base these changes on greater self-knowledge.

The ability to react to stress emotionally, to come apart, and then to pull oneself together again is the heart of the creative process—a process that requires calling upon important inner resources as they are needed.

Our Inner Resources

When the philosopher and theologian Martin Buber spoke of the importance of the "I" in the I-Thou relationship, he was referring to what psychological theory calls the ego, or consciousness, the sense of self. This is the set of functions that reasons, perceives the reality around us and the reality within us, remembers, forgets, makes decisions, unmakes them, interprets for us what we are, and integrates the various components of the personality to provide a sense of security and fulfillment.

The Need for a Strong Ego

We educate the ego. We teach it how to read and write, to count and multiply, to think logically and abstractly, to judge and apply values.

There are certain important stages in the formation of a healthy ego. One of the most critical is the resolution of narcissism—overvaluation of the self. It is a commonly accepted theory that infants experience themselves as all-powerful and all-knowing—and who is to say that, in their own way, they are not? As they are bumped around, by parents and especially by other children who shout, "It's mine, it's mine," they are forced to reconsider who and what they are. Normally, they emerge from this set of events realizing that they are not the center of the world and gradually relinquishing their narcissism. Unfortunately, some children come out of this crisis with a reverse type of narcissism and feel that, when all is said and done, they really amount to nothing.

To attain a strong and active ego requires a successful resolution of the problem of narcissism. As the existential psychoanalyst Rollo May points out: "When an individual insists on his or her own subjectivity and follows exclusively his or her own imagination, we have a person whose flights of fancy may be interesting but who never really relates to the objective world." A well-functioning ego permits us to accept realistic limits and, at the same time, regard ourselves as special. In this way growing children and, later, adults can take themselves sufficiently for granted to channel their energies and affections into people and things outside themselves. And they can do so with a genuine commitment, free of any residual compulsion to restore their original sense of omnipotence or to confirm their worthlessness, as the case may be.

Psychiatrist Karl Menninger calls the ego "the guardian of the vital balance." A strong ego—which is by no means an inflexible one—is essential to the adaptive process of falling apart and recovering again. People who are too tightly put together usually cannot adjust to changing conditions. They feel threatened by "openness," whether to ideas, other people, or their own unconscious resources. Such a lack of resilience often passes for strength of character, when, in fact, it is both an obstacle to the individual's capacity for growth and, frequently, a reflection of the amount of internal chaos and disturbance that exists within the unconscious, over which control must be maintained at all times.

That the ego should be resilient does not imply a chameleonlike quality, an indiscriminate shifting of color as situations change. It means that new information and new experiences can penetrate the person's consciousness and that the conflict which may result between the new and old can be resolved and lead to a worthwhile synthesis. By the same token, a poorly developed ego—one that lacks organization and discipline—will have a hard time of it when faced with any kind of stress and the need to respond creatively.

The Nature of the Unconscious

To think and act creatively requires a well-put-together personality; it calls for an effective balance between the ego and the resources of the unconscious. The popular concept of the unconscious is oversimplified and its nature much misunderstood. It is commonly seen as a murky area where all kinds of malevolent and destructive motivations reside, ready to take over at any time. In fact, not only is the unconscious complex, with many characteristics and levels, but it can be a major ally in life. It is, among other things, the site of creative thinking.

That every person has an unconscious is now generally accepted. And we know that complete release from repression of what the unconscious contains will lead to madness. It is in the hospitals for the seriously mentally ill that we see the most extreme openness of contact between consciousness and the drives and impulses of the unconscious. The function of an intact ego is not only to keep the unconscious from intruding in unwanted and disruptive ways, but also to permit access to its contents as we need them.

As a parent watching small children grow, I have felt definite moments of sadness that so many of the happy experiences which take place will never be recalled. It is as if nature deemed it necessary, for whatever reason, to eliminate forever the details of the first years of life by failing to provide the neural structure that would be required for such recall. But perhaps, on the other hand, the brain must be able to shut out certain perceptions from consciousness in order for us to function.

The English philosopher C. D. Broad, in discussing the theories of Henri Bergson, suggested that

> the function of the brain and nervous system and sense organs is in the main eliminative and not productive. Each person is at each moment capable of remembering all that has ever happened to him and of perceiving everything that is happening everywhere in the universe. The function of the brain and nervous system is to protect us from being overwhelmed and confused by this mass of largely useless and irrelevant knowledge . . . leaving only that very small and special selection which is likely to be practically useful.

The concept of the unconscious was central to early psychoanalytic theory, which postulated that the personality could be divided into three important parts: the ego, or the conscious self; the id, which was largely unconscious and contained the early archaic residue of childhood rage and sexuality; and the superego, which contained the conscience—the arbiter of right and wrong—and also the personal ideals and expectations that one should try to live up to. Those whose superegos were too strongly developed would be inhibited by unhealthy guilt and plagued with a sense of failure and a tendency to punish themselves for things over which they had no control. Those who had insufficient control over the forces of the unconscious or who were being unduly influenced by them would develop a variety of behavioral problems, from impulsive, self-destructive actions to outright psychosis.

As the theory and practice of psychoanalysis expanded, the nature of the balance between the conscious self and the unconscious became a major focus of interest. The goal of analysis was to free the patient from the hold that unconscious forces had over him. "Where Id was," said Freud, "there Ego shall be." By this he meant that the unconscious, as he envisioned it, would have less of a hold on one's ability to function, being replaced by an expanded consciousness and, with it, the dominance of reason.

America adopted its own interpretation of the unconscious with a passion. Sociologist John Seeley, in *The Americanization of the Unconscious*, described this phenomenon. In the classroom, for example,

> everything is seen, "understood," and acted upon (as far as reality permits) in terms of the depth drama actually or possibly underlying any act. Little behavior is taken at face value; almost without consciousness of alternative possibil-

ities of perception, everything very neatly is "interpreted." The role of the teacher as a "parent-surrogate" is understood and accepted. It is expected that "hostility" will be "displaced" upon her, that drawings, essays, polite exchanges have "covert" meanings much different from their "overt" content—and much more real and much more interesting. The "libidinal" give and take that accompanies all communication (or motivates it?) is noted, albeit less easily accepted. If Johnny throws a spit-ball at Mary, nothing so ordinary as "mischief" is afoot.

While the point of view that minimizes conscious factors in motivation and assumes the individual to be helpless in the face of such hidden purposes is clearly exaggerated and portrays the unconscious in a singularly unfavorable light, the influence of the unconscious on thinking and behavior, for good or ill, should never be overlooked.

Psychological theory has envisioned the unconscious in various ways. One of the main subjects of Freud's theories was the deeper and highly personal unconscious. Within it there are things about ourselves of which we are not aware, things that are virtually inaccessible because they are stored deep in the repository of early experiences, memories, thoughts, desires. Here they simmer away —unresolved, timeless, primitive, and powerful in influencing our current perceptions and behavior.

How is this part of the unconscious formed? The child, growing up, is not only involved in the process of learning how to speak, how to differentiate colors and shapes, and how to play games, but is also laying down highly charged impressions of self and reality that will constitute the deeper levels of the unconscious for years to come. There is every reason to assume that these premises are being imprinted on the very substance of the brain tissues and will remain there, active, defying logic, and affecting adult perceptions in spite of anything that may happen afterward.

Psychoanalyst Erik Erikson has offered one of the clearest definitions of the relationship between the early childhood experiences that contribute to the kind of unconscious a person constructs and the adult attitudes that person will develop. The nature of the interaction between the mother and the infant, he stated, is critical in creating a healthy sense of trust. From this interaction the infant forms "the springs of the basic sense of trust and the basic sense of mistrust which remain the autogenic source of both primal hope and of doom throughout life."

We may conclude, then, that if early life experiences are supportive and constructive, the deeper unconscious will work to the individual's benefit. If, on the other hand, one's early life experiences are troubled and traumatic, its influence may prove destructive, impairing one's ability to perceive things as they are and paralyzing one's freedom to respond creatively to stress.

One divorced woman regularly and harshly criticized her former husband as being a poor father, in spite of the fact that he had been more than adequately attentive to the needs of their children, supporting them financially and spending a great deal of time with them as well. She was not simply trying to upset him; she really believed, at those moments, that what she was saying was true. Whatever he might have done for their children in recent years was totally unavailable to her recall. The underlying motive in her accusations could be understood only by appreciating the perceptions buried more deeply in her unconscious.

Her own father had deserted her mother when she was two years old. When she was ten, her mother married a man who treated the girl and her sisters with blatant cruelty. The concept that a father was at best unreliable and at worst brutal was so strongly fixed in this woman's mind that, regardless of the events and experiences of her adult years, she chose only her former husband's failures and shortcomings to remember and dismissed his good qualities from her awareness.

This deeper unconscious with its dark and sinister overtones is what commonly comes to mind when the broad term "unconscious" is mentioned. I recall having during my own psychoanalysis what Freud would have undoubtedly classified as an Oedipal dream: a nightmare in which my father literally evaporated and was replaced by a young, attractive, and extremely seductive woman whom I knew casually. I was startled by the implication of an intense link between my attraction to this woman and a deeply buried irrational and destructive impulse toward my father. The analyst seemed pleased, but even to this day I am not sure whether dream truly reflected the conflict it suggested or whether, since I was already steeped in psychoanalytic theory, I dreamed it to accommodate the analytic situation or perhaps the analyst himself.

The Preconscious: Where Creative Thinking Takes Place

Freud, however, must be given credit for formulating another facet of the unconscious: the preconscious, which Lawrence Kubie was the first to envision as the major site of creative thinking. Not only experiences of early childhood are forgotten, but also innumerable events that take place later in childhood and even in adolescent and adult years. Memories of the more recent events are usually more accessible to recall than those buried in the deeper unconscious and are therefore considered to be in the preconscious. However, in addition to being filled with information, feelings, and perceptions which shape our reactions to what we experience, the preconscious is also a place where things actually happen.

Logical, analytic, and highly structured thinking, valuable as it may be in the earlier and later stages of creative thinking, is often a major obstacle to the discovery of new viewpoints. In the creative process, during the phase of incubation, ordinary reasoning has to be temporarily suspended to allow new ideas to be born. Their birth takes place within the preconscious. There, with incredible speed and without the constrictions of ordinary logic, we can sift through data and connect contradictory concepts in order to form new ideas. The preconscious has the power to mobilize large quantities of such data rapidly and efficiently and find interrelationships between dissimilar ingredients to build new conceptual and perceptual patterns. Here we can move experiences about and combine them in fantastic ways.

Experimental hypermnesia—the intensified ability to recall observations under hypnosis—confirms this ability. If one is asked to observe various objects in a room and then recall them, and later is hypnotized, thereby tapping the preconscious, one can, under the influence of hypnosis, remember nearly ten times the number of details that could be recalled on a purely conscious level.

Values and the Collective Unconscious

There is another concept of the unconscious which is critical to creativity. Carl Jung proposed that in each of us there exists an impersonal part of the unconscious. This part, unrelated to our own life experiences, is carried forward, like a balance on a ledger sheet, from prior generations. This is the collective unconscious, which is made up of the essence of those human experiences that have been repeated often enough and have been formative enough over the millenniums of man's existence to cause a permanent, although not necessarily unalterable, imprint on the neural structure. Perhaps carried by way of the genes, this collective unconscious contains concepts and perceptions of a universal nature, having to do with the survival and evolution of mankind itself. Jung called these "archetypal sources" and described them as being concerned with such universal human experiences as mothering, fathering, femininity, masculinity, strength, responsibility, good and evil, home.

For many years I experienced a recurrent dream, the contents of which must have originated in my own collective unconscious. In the dream I kept searching for a particular room in a particular house. It was one of those large old frame houses one sees along the New Jersey coast or on Cape Cod, built in the early part of this century and used as summer retreats. There were two houses in the dream. I always found one, but I could not, however hard I tried, find the second. Each time I awoke feeling disappointed, frustrated, and unfulfilled.

Then one night I actually found the second house, and

the room as well. Its appearance is hazy in my mind, but there was a strong sense of familiarity about it, and the feeling that went along with the discovery still remains vivid—a feeling of home, of settling, of coming to terms with and resolving some long-standing condition of turmoil and confusion. This was the last time I had the dream, and the experience corresponded in time to the end of a long period of personal and professional uprooting, when things were beginning to straighten out, and confirmed my conscious sense that I was once again moving in the right direction.

Although I agree with Kubie that the preconscious is the chief mechanism involved in the creative process, I am convinced that it is the collective part of the unconscious which lends validity and credence to the new ideas and options that emerge. Here lie the ethical and universal elements of every important idea, however personal, we discover, because this is where we are most in touch with the laws of nature, even when we are unable to formulate these in conscious thoughts or words.

What concerns me, after years of practicing therapy, is the extent to which we seem to have lost touch with the guidelines contained in the collective unconscious. Instead, as external constraints to behavior have been removed, we have become more vulnerable to motivations that originate in the deeper and more personal unconscious. In fact, the very balance between consciousness and the unconscious has shifted, to such an extent that what appeared to constitute the "stuff" of the unconscious in Freud's time seems today to have surfaced and to be quite apparent in the conscious thoughts and behavior of many people. In contrast, many elements—such as the belief in, and respect for, certain values—which were formerly quite conscious and which were taken for granted a generation ago, seem to have been pushed down into the unconscious. Instead of discovering within the unconscious of a tense, tightly controlled person clues that point to sexual confusion—a man's urge to dress up in his mother's clothes, for example—it is far more likely today that the transvestism will be found right there in the open for all to see. On the other hand, facets of the personality that were quite apparent years ago—ideals, sense of purpose, hero images—appear to have been buried, along with such traditional values as a sense of justice or an understanding of personal courage.

Freud's promise was that "where Id was, there Ego shall be," but the result of his efforts seems to be "where Superego was, there Id is." Our current culture has somehow provided a climate in which Freud's Id, with all its sexual and aggressive components, has emerged in full force. And the shift in the balance, rather than supplying a higher degree of personal consciousness and freedom, has more often shut out one's sense of purpose and idealism. As the cover of *New York* magazine pointedly asked, referring to an article entitled "The Missing American Hero," "Where are you, Gary Cooper, now that we need you?"

A rearrangement in this balance is obviously required, with insight into ourselves and into our world as a vital part of that rearrangement.

8
The *Equus* Dilemma

In Peter Shafer's controversial play, *Equus,* the characters
are faced with some difficult choices. The psychiatrist
engaged in treating the boy who blinded the horses—an
act presumably caused by sexual confusion and guilt—is
himself caught in the middle of a personal crisis, confronted with what he feels to be the hollowness of his life
and reluctant to cure his patient because of the consequences he envisions as inseparable from that cure: Take
away the boy's madness and you destroy his uniqueness.
Wreck his illusions and you subject him to a life of tedium
and anonymity. Help him to gain some degree of insight
into what he is experiencing and why, and to restore his
ability to cope with reality, and you will rob him of his
creativeness.

Playwrights are not alone in criticizing insight. Psychiatrist Arnold Pearce, writing for the British medical journal
Lancet, stated that

the widespread belief that insight, like a much advertised alcoholic beverage, is good for you and that you cannot have too much of it certainly requires qualification. Carried to logical absurdity we should all be so busy trying to find out what makes us tick that we should never have the time to tick at all.

The case against insight is well entrenched. "What you don't know won't hurt you" and "What's the good in realizing something you can't do anything about?" and "If I analyze every thought and motivation inside me, I'll never get anything done and only get confused" are but a few of the objections one commonly hears. In a series of full-page advertisements for a book on transcendental meditation (and without doing justice to the potential in meditation), the copywriters tacitly acknowledged the public's reluctance to work at increasing self-knowledge by suggesting that reading the book could help one learn how to relieve anxieties and the impact of stress almost without effort—meaning, of course, without insight.

Psychiatrists and behavioral scientists did not invent either the concept or the term "insight." In fact, they have often taken steps to avoid defining it, and if one looks through the indexes of the majority of books in these fields, more often than not the term does not appear at all. It has been treated like the word "income," which has never been defined in the Internal Revenue Code. Even though the Supreme Court wrestled with a definition of income in 1921, it failed to arrive at a satisfactory solution, and to this day the word remains without clarification, lest it immediately open itself up to misinterpretation, troublesome loopholes, unwanted restrictions.

To gain insight is simply to become aware of some salient fact about ourselves that we had not been conscious of before, to look at someone else or some aspect of external reality in a different way. Insight involves a change in perception, a significant change in perspective, a heightening of consciousness that requires forfeiting an old way of viewing something in favor of a new and more accurate one.

Such an increase in awareness can be an intellectual experience, or a very real alteration in the way in which one sees and feels reality, or both. Many people who read Freud or Jung or books on transactional analysis—or popular interpretations of all these—merely acquire a new terminology for defining their problems without any additional ability to resolve the problems themselves.

Hundreds of people have undergone traditional psychoanalysis five times a week for three or more years, and have emerged with little more than a new vocabulary to describe what they think about themselves and others. "My tendency to put off things and my laziness is actually a form of masochism," said one man who had been through eight years of analysis, "and it comes from the abusive attitude which my mother had toward me, toward my father, toward all men. But so what? I still can't get started doing things—I still don't have any energy. What good did all this probing do? What was the point?"

Insights That Count

Knowledge by itself is not without value. The term insight, however, should be reserved for those changes in perception that affect the total personality, that permit a genuinely fresh appraisal of whatever the issue may be, and that lead to the creation of a fundamentally different state of mind. Something new should be added, producing a change, both conscious and unconscious, in the way people experience themselves.

Psychotherapy, even when it consists of only a few sessions, is one setting in which such changes can occur. "I had been dragging myself around for a couple of years," one patient said. "Couldn't sleep well. Was tired most of the time. Had no energy. I didn't want to go anywhere or see anybody, but I would force myself to keep doing things, hoping that whatever it was would go away. At first I thought that it must be some physical problem. A complete checkup with my doctor and several more visits produced absolutely nothing. Finally, in desperation, I agreed to see a psychiatrist. After only four visits, I could feel my energy coming back. I was less frightened. For two reasons, I think. For the first time I realized that what I had been going through was something which could be understood and which a doctor could help me with. And secondly, rather than being something that just appeared gratuitously, out of the blue, I was able to tie it into a period of my life, three years before, when I had been going through a hell of a lot of stress. My father had died. My wife and I were having a lot of trouble with our seventeen-year-old son. I was reaching forty. Suddenly it all made sense. The frightening illogicality of it all was removed and I could actually feel the fear beginning to drain away."

The confusion between intellectual knowledge and the experience of insight has caused psychiatrists and others to disagree vehemently over the merit of the latter. Some feel that insight has no bearing on the ultimate outcome of psychotherapy. There are patients who can put into words all kinds of explanations for their distress and still feel no improvement, while others become free of symptoms and function more effectively without ever being able to explain the nature of the change they have gone through. Many psychiatrists, however, believe that only through an increase in awareness and a change in perspective can a patient resolve inner conflicts or come to terms with the environment.

This dispute results in no small measure from too narrow a definition of insight; namely, that it consists of seeing oneself and one's life in terms of a particular psychological theory—that one's ambition to succeed in business, for example, is really a compensation for an early childhood castration anxiety. Thus a relatively simple insight, such as realizing that you fail to set limits on the extent to which other people invade your living space and control you, would not be considered a true insight within, in this case, the Freudian psychoanalytic construct. Nevertheless, for many people such an awareness can produce a major shift in the equilibrium within which they live.

A second assumption that derives from psychoanalytic theory, with its pessimistic and deterministic overtones, is the fear that any awareness gained is bound to shed some highly unpleasant light on one's character, that behind one's seemingly most innocent conscious urges lurk sinister and unattractive instincts, that one's spiritual convictions, for instance, are really a "masochistic" sublimation of infantile masturbatory impulses, or that one's enjoyment in teaching is really a substitute for childhood exhibitionism.

On the contrary, the realizations that we gain can equally often lead to the recognition and release of constructive forces and motivations which, for a variety of reasons, have been neglected or forgotten. The perspective one has had about one's past can shift.

"I've always hung onto bad memories of my childhood," a woman patient reported. "Memories of my parents screaming at me and at each other, of my being unhappy and wanting desperately to get away from home at thirteen, fourteen. I started to distort the past when I went away to college. It was part of breaking away, growing up. But before I ever worked it out and regained perspective, I married a man my family disapproved of. For twenty years I felt I had to choose him over them, and to justify my choice I had to keep alive an image of them as insensitive and without understanding. It was only after our divorce that I could reappraise my family and realize that my life at home had little connection with the image I had created and forced myself to retain."

Spurs to Insight

It is no coincidence that the development of insight is triggered by a shift in one's equilibrium—a stress —significant enough to induce pain. Much of the time we go along reasonably contented or explaining our discontent in terms which, though frequently incorrect, seem to make sense to us. An inertia, common to all of us, whispers: Leave well enough alone. Whatever our attitudes or patterns of behavior, they are more likely to persist, unchanged, than to disappear or be replaced by different ones. If, for example, we are overly permissive with our children or bored by our work or feel put upon by our husbands or wives, the chances are that we will not do anything about changing the situation or the way in which we experience the situation until something happens of a sufficiently disturbing nature to hurt or upset us profoundly. And even then we will not act unless we recognize that we are hurting, psychologically.

Depression has been described as a form of hurting that is triggered by a change involving the loss of someone or something we value. This feeling of hopelessness, futility, fear should alert us to the need for insight and change. But it is more than a signal. It is often an inherent part of the process of first coming apart and then recovering with new insight, and hence with a new level of consciousness, when this shift means giving up an old perspective that had been a significant aspect of the way in which we viewed ourselves. Moreover, we often feel a lowering in self-esteem and a sense of regret when the new insight permits us to see the mistakes we have made, how we might have handled situations differently, more successfully, in the past, how we might have found greater fulfillment over the years now gone.

Let us assume, for example, that you have spent thirty years of your life operating on the premise: "I don't trust anyone, nor has anyone given me any reason to trust them." This assumption will have given you a somewhat jaundiced view of life, a continual underlying sense of insecurity, and will have encouraged you to keep a safe distance between yourself and others. The result may have been loneliness. On many occasions you may really have needed the support of someone else but would not or could not reach out to anyone. You might have rationalized your premise quite well or even inadvertently sought out relationships that afford plenty of evidence of disappointments or betrayals to confirm it. The realization that your assumption is invalid—that there are some people you can learn to trust, even though there are others whom, for good reasons, you should not trust—cannot be reached painlessly. At some point you must confront yourself with the lost opportunities for closeness, with the poor judgment you have shown in choosing people to associate with—in work, or in love relationships—who only reinforced your assumption, and with the recollection of the many times you could have weathered difficult situations more successfully had there been at least one person to rely on and share things with. Facing such an awareness cannot but be, for a while, depressing.

But as time passes, whether weeks or perhaps months, and as the new way of looking at things settles in, is tested, and works, a sense of freedom and renewal takes over. A sense of wholeness results.

Several years ago, I attended a weekend conference at the Bucks County Seminar House, a training session in meditation led by author Alan Watts. I was motivated partly by curiosity and partly by a conviction that what for me was a totally unfamiliar kind of experience might help to stimulate creativity.

At one point during the weekend we were asked to look at objects around us, such as the texture of the barn walls, the sky as seen through an opening in the roof, to listen to the sound of the wind and the birds, and to refrain from defining any of these objects in language. We were not to think of the sky as sky, or blue, or far away, or to think of the sounds of the birds as bird-sounds, but rather to allow ourselves to perceive each of these things in a direct and immediate manner, as if for the first time ever, before any words had been given to them.

At once I became aware of the extent to which my intellectual habits of analyzing, categorizing, evaluating—the very skills that had been emphasized and sharpened throughout medical school—had also worked to block out the direct perception of sights and sounds as they really were. The process of excessively logical thinking had cut me off from sharp contact with my environment and diminished the receptivity I might otherwise have had to immediate intuitive messages. A new channel for communication between my conscious self and my preconscious opened, and my confidence in my own intuition was significantly reinforced. And with this came, as well, a greater sense of personal freedom.

The reintegrative phase of gaining insight does not always occur so quickly. It may take place gradually. A woman may react almost automatically with nervousness and impatience to any show of insecurity or low spirits in her husband; this is not what she expects of him, and it makes her feel personally threatened. She may then begin to reconsider her response, seeing how it makes her husband withdraw from her or leads to pointless arguing. For a while, her new point of view conflicts with her old one. She tries to be more understanding and accepting, but her feelings fail to follow. She has to make a deliberate effort to conceal them, or, in expressing them, to admit to her unreasonableness. She may even try to inject some humor into the situation, to dilute the impact. Eventually, over a period of time, she discovers a new sense of empathy that emerges spontaneously as a genuine part of herself.

This gradual change is what the therapist commonly encounters in his work. One patient noted, after I had pointed out a previously unrecognized motive in his behavior: "I've thought about this pattern of sloppy work at school and later on at the job as a way of getting back at my parents. I used to think I was just inadequate, or at least unmotivated. This is a new idea and I don't know what to do with it."

This patient was a young businessman who had started treatment because of periods of depression, a pattern of job instability, and periodic episodes of high blood pressure. The new perspective seemed alien to him. It seemed artificial. It certainly did not bring about any significant change in his behavior or mood at first. Months later, however, he commented, "I'm beginning to feel a difference. That idea suddenly rings true. I don't know why now, why not when you first brought it up. But I'm finding myself doing fewer and fewer things to screw up, things that used to provoke the people I work with, like being late and not having reports in on time, and doing more with the feeling that I'm in command of myself."

It is common in psychotherapy to see patients initially doubt or reject new insights, sometimes angrily. This denial is frequently followed by a period of distress and, to some degree, of falling apart. Then the point is actively reconsidered by the patient, and he or she finds that it has a validity it had previously lacked. Still further down the road, patients may even forget the particular insights that have been the prime catalysts for the new sense of freedom and energy. As the equilibrium restores itself, the new way of thinking, being, acting, has a naturalness and unself-consciousness about it—a sharp contrast to the myth that increased awareness leads to a morbid and paralyzing self-preoccupation.

Some people have more innate ability than others to synthesize new experiences and points of view. The traditional psychoanalytic model requires the patient to have a high degree of reintegrative ability, since the analyst plays a more passive and uninvolved role in the procedure. A more active therapist will often assist the patient in putting the pieces together again and will also help that person learn some of the techniques of synthesis, so that after therapy the patient will be able to do more of this alone as new situations require it. The absence of this important step of reintegration is the factor that has made the experience of therapy, for so many people, little more than an elaborate dissection.

A genuine experience of insight results in a very real change in attitudes or behavior patterns, as exemplified by the individuals who forfeit the need to control others as a means of protection against an unfounded, inner sense of

danger; those who, having realized that they had been
inhibited in giving of themselves to others because they
feared rejection, can begin to show—gingerly at first, later
more spontaneously—how much they care for those for
whom they do care; those whose blood pressure returns to
a lower level once they stop trying to cram in more than
they can do in a limited period of time and learn how to
protect themselves by setting limits on family and friends
who take advantage of them, instead of allowing frustration
and then rage to build up internally. All these people can
be said to have gained a meaningful, workable insight that
has released them to approach life with new energy and
sense of purpose.

Psychiatrists themselves particularly need to develop a
capacity for insight. This is one reason why so many go
through psychoanalysis: to put themselves in better contact
with their own feelings and motivations; to loosen up the
boundaries of their personalities, permitting a freer flow
between the conscious and the unconscious; to reduce the
controls which the deeper levels of the unconscious have
over them. All this should ultimately strengthen their ability to deal with the wide variety of situations presented to
them by their patients.

For example, therapists must develop insight into their
own aggressive and hostile emotions. In my own experience, although I knew that many of my patients had difficulty in recognizing and managing angry feelings—some
did not know that they were angry when they were angry,
others suppressed anger as a matter of policy, others found
it difficult to control—it took me a number of years to

translate what I observed in them into a new insight that worked for myself. I had always tried to maintain good relationships with people, but in the process of doing so, I tended to suppress my angry feelings, often beyond awareness. To avoid controversy, I allowed others to intrude unreasonably on territory that was, so to speak, legitimately mine, accepting such invasions as philosophically as possible. Constantly working with patients who had similar difficulties eventually forced me to reconsider my own reactions.

At first, I found myself veering to the opposite extreme of losing my temper immediately when provoked. Sometimes this was justifiable; at other times it was not. Then I learned that in certain situations losing my temper not only produced desired results but also cleared the air. And finally, I learned how to avoid unnecessary opportunities for anger by dealing with things sooner and setting limits on the extent to which various people might step in on me, out of either self-interest or thoughtlessness.

Cybernetics, a concept that deals with "open" and "closed" systems, viewing human behavior as an open system, offers a theoretical framework for such an experience. It describes how a state of equilibrium can be restored at a higher level after it has been shaken up by change. During the reintegrative stage, as learning proceeds, one tends to overdo and underdo the job alternately, like the swinging of a pendulum. If, for example, you have decided to show openly a greater degree of affection to someone you love, whereas previously you had been very self-conscious and constricted about such expression of feeling, you may well touch, cling, kiss, and hug at times in a clumsy way. Your demonstrativeness might sometimes be carried to excess or sometimes be poorly timed. You might periodically withdraw until you learn how to feel comfortable with the new kind of behavior.

Even a temporary imbalance of this kind is not well tolerated by a person whose mind is closed, who must always be right. In a marriage, for example, when one or the other partner seems incapable of going through such a process, issues cannot be reconsidered, communication dwindles, and a mood of "quiet desperation" sets in, which even the most skilled marital therapy can rarely reverse.

Insights: What to Look For

The insights that are needed in order to adjust to various life situations and stresses will obviously depend on what those situations are and on the total life experience of the person up to that point. In all of us, certain aspects of the personality are more finely developed than others; some have been relatively neglected. Only children, for example, often set high standards for themselves and may be strongly motivated to succeed. A great many senior executives in major corporations and successful professional people are only children. However, there is often a gap in the development of only children which results from the lack of brothers and sisters with whom, in ordinary give and take, they could have learned how to set limits on personal expectations. They are likely to feel that whatever they have accomplished is never quite enough. They are often deprived of a sufficient degree of personal gratification from what they have done and find it difficult throughout their lives to engage in fulfilling relationships with their contemporaries. By contrast, there are those who, having grown up in large families and mastered many of the fundamentals of interpersonal relationships, still have not learned how to overcome conflicts about competitiveness or to resist pressures to conform to standards set by friends or society in general. Only children are often more capable of withstanding such pressures, since these have much less importance for them. In either case different insights are required to meet different demands.

Regardless of our backgrounds, however, we all have a common stress to face which only the ability to form new perceptions can meet—a Kantian world in which the differences in the way people see and react to reality have become increasingly striking. Subjectivity rules, as if the perceptions themselves' defined reality and reality had no properties of its own. We have been set adrift, left extensively to our own devices to distinguish between what is real and what is not. External guidelines evaporate. Each of us is left to judge and live by values which we ourselves concoct, in a "you do your thing and I'll do mine" kind of world. What this means, from a practical viewpoint, is that consensus about anything is harder and harder to obtain. There is the constant risk of projecting inner conflicts and problems onto the environment in a vain effort to solve through action what can only be resolved from within.

Becoming more aware has become a prerequisite for survival as an individual. Fortunately, during the last few decades, and in spite of the popularity of deceptively easy solutions to complex human problems, there has been a growing recognition of the importance of insight, along with the development of a variety of new ways to increase self-knowledge.

9
Blindfolds and
Other Aids to Vision

At the end of Plato's *Apology,* his defense of his teacher,
Socrates, Socrates says, "The hour of departure has arrived, and we go our ways—I to die, and you to live.
Which is better is known only to the gods." I was sixteen
when I studied the *Apology* in Greek class. The professor,
an intense, dedicated man in his early seventies—reminis-
cent of James Hilton's Mr. Chips—read this final section
aloud in the original Greek at the last session of the class,
and as he read, tears formed in his eyes.

He had been teaching this subject for nearly fifty years. I
could not be sure just what he was responding to—Socrates' courage, the essential wisdom in the text, its drama, or
the fact that this was to be our last meeting. The course
was ending, and perhaps his teaching career, and most
certainly his relationship with me and the four other students in the program. I can only say that then and even
now, looking back, the moment carried with it a whole
cluster of insights too complex to explain fully, but includ-

ing a profound realization that there is nothing un-
masculine about tears; that to show feeling when a situation merits feeling is indeed a mark of maturity; that truth
and integrity are values worth striving for; that an old man
with compassion could inspire us with words spoken more
than two thousand years ago; that ideas can be the most
powerful force in the world.

The most important source of insight is living—those
experiences that bring us together, in a moment of time,
with some person, some set of circumstances that afford us
a new way of seeing ourselves and our worlds.

Readiness to Change

Events collaborate periodically in the lives of each of us
to deepen our insight—if we are ready. Readiness, as emphasized by the Swiss psychologist Jean Piaget in his work
on perception, is a special openness and willingness to listen and learn. Unfortunately, such openness is not always
within reach, and it cannot be created simply by an act of
will. Psychotherapies, including psychoanalysis—more
formal approaches to the acquisition of insight—are themselves as much a preparation for a change in perception as
they are a way of transmitting any particular collection of
insights.

"Are you going to tell me something about myself I
don't already know?" is a common question raised by people in therapy. The therapist might well answer, "That, or
a new way of looking at what you already know, but only
when you become ready to see and understand." What
must take place first is a reduction in those vested interests
that keep us from looking at ourselves differently.

Sometimes such readiness is forced on us, painfully, by outside circumstances. As one man described it: "I had been going along in this business, trying to get contracts to make commercial films for companies, for nearly ten years. The first two or three went extremely well. We had plenty of work. After that competition got stiffer. Also, I wasn't about to fool around with kickbacks and a lot of other things going on. I felt that the quality of what we produced could speak for itself. Anyway, we limped along for another seven years. I had to borrow to keep going and to meet living expenses. My wife kept telling me to get out of it, but I wouldn't listen. I blamed her for not giving me the moral support I needed.

"Finally, last summer, the banks called my loans. Interest rates were up. I wasn't that good a customer and they wanted cash. I was literally forced out of business. But I can see, now, that I was also forced to come to my senses. I was a lousy businessman, frankly, but I wasn't willing to admit that to myself. Whatever those skills or instincts are that give someone in business the right sense of risk-taking, the right sense of how not to overextend his resources, of how to cut his losses, of the best approach to selling—I didn't have them. In the beginning, I had come up with some new ideas in a good and receptive economy. But when things got rougher, I couldn't make it. But I couldn't accept not making it, either.

"Before going into this kind of work I had been very successful in the creative side of a first-rate advertising agency. Friends of mine had left to go into business for themselves. I thought I could do it too. But it's one thing to let someone else worry about balancing budgets while you come up with ideas, and quite another to try to do both for yourself, at least for someone like me. I can't understand numbers, don't even like to think about money. Maybe I could have changed this attitude, but I didn't try. I wasn't motivated to try. I didn't even see its relevance.

"I was lucky. Once I was forced to come to terms with myself, by simple economics, I was able to get a pretty good job again, doing the only thing I do best. I sleep better, my relationship with my family is better, every day isn't a constant round of frustrations and fears."

Whether triggered by circumstances or initiated by something within oneself, the process of gaining insight is easily catalyzed by reviewing the issues with another person. This requires trust in the listener, who must acknowledge that it is your perspective that needs to be reordered—not simply replaced by his own, even when he can and should draw on his knowledge and experience to help you make such a shift. It is also essential that the listener recognize that some degree of falling apart will take place before you can pull yourself together again and that you need, perhaps more than anything, active and compassionate support to understand the anguish and the feeling of being lost or confused that you may experience in transit.

This is one of the reasons, though certainly not the only one, for the development of formal counseling and psychotherapy. Psychoanalysis in particular was evolved for the purpose of making an individual achieve a maximum degree of insight which would lead, in turn, to a rebalancing of the relationship between the conscious and unconscious.

The process of opening up was catalyzed by the technique referred to as free association. Free association—putting into words those thoughts and feelings that occur to a person spontaneously, as they emerge, without regard for the logical processes of thought—was by no means original with Freud. It is essentially the experience of verbalizing random thoughts in a stream of consciousness. The poet Friedrich Schiller, in a letter in 1788, recommended this method to anyone who wished to be productive. The English philosopher Thomas Hobbes, in his *Leviathan* (1651), stated:

> When a man thinketh on any thing whatsoever, His next Thought after, is not altogether so casual as it seems to be. Not every Thought to every Thought succeeds indifferently. . . . And yet in this wild ranging of the mind, a man may oft-times perceive the way of it, and the dependence of one Thought upon another.

The actual events that transpire within psychoanalysis are far more complex than this—involving, for example, such phenomena as transference, wherein the subject of the analysis re-experiences in the relationship with the therapist basic drives and feelings that derive from earlier relationships in life, especially those of the formative childhood years. But the discovery of those unconscious forces that operate within the individual and influence him or her in unseen ways is activated by means of free association. What takes place is an unstructuring in the logical processes of thinking, in what is called the "secondary process." Temporarily deferring judgment and evaluation allows the elements of the "primary," or unconscious, process to come out. Theoretically, their force can thereby be minimized, and as they return again to the unconscious, the individual will discover greater freedom from what may have been their excessive influence.

A curious and common misunderstanding about psychoanalysis, in its traditional, classic form, deserves mention. Because analysis is so costly and takes so much time—often four or five sessions a week for several years—the natural assumption is that a person would have to be pretty unbalanced to require such intensive work. Paradoxically, the very opposite is true. Probing the unconscious in this way requires, if anything, a well-integrated yet flexible personality so that the individual can tolerate the periods of disruption and incoherence that necessarily accompany the process. Moreover, people must have the strength and resilience to synthesize the experience and pull themselves together again. Hence it is less a treatment for those in acute distress than for those who are already in fairly good shape but for whom some kind of pain has stimulated a need for greater awareness and for strengthening, perhaps by loosening up, an already strong personality.

Resistance

The term "resistance" was coined in the early days of psychoanalysis to describe those forces in the personality that fight against insight. Resistance is not, by and large, a conscious act. It has nothing to do with being cooperative or uncooperative. It is automatic. It is a more or less conditioned response, serving the purpose of preserving the status quo, the equilibrium in the way we presently view ourselves. It is also a response designed to avoid the anxiety and helplessness that go along with letting down our guard long enough to permit what is beyond awareness to emerge.

"I found it very difficult to accept the fact that I had handled my marriage poorly," commented one thirty-four year-old woman. "I blamed my husband instead. I could avoid coming to terms with myself as long as I could accuse him of being the cause of our problems. During therapy, I felt angry whenever the psychiatrist attempted to suggest that I might have been contributing to the situation. More than once, I almost quit therapy. Obviously, even though I refused to see it, criticizing his apparent inadequacies all the time made him relatively impotent. Admitting this would have made me feel like a failure, one-down somehow, and responsible in a way I didn't want to face. It's as if to acknowledge that I was doing something wrong, making a series of mistakes, would be a dangerous thing, like opening a Pandora's box of ugly self-questioning. To think well of myself, I had to go on destroying my marriage rather than rethink what I was doing and change."

Resistance, however, also serves a constructive purpose. It fosters intactness by keeping too much of one's unconscious from intruding upon one's ability to function and handle day-to-day realities. "What exactly would it mean," asks anthropologist Ernest Becker in *The Denial of Death*, ". . . to be wholly unrepressed, to live in full bodily and psychic expansiveness?" It could only "mean to be reborn into madness." Without character traits which carry with them limitations on insight and awareness, there would be "full and open psychosis."

Many people, in trying through various consciousness-raising experiences to become more aware of forgotten and repressed elements within them while at the same time ignoring both the inherent resistances that exist within everyone, and the insecurity and disorganization that must accompany such a search, have only come upon further personal chaos.

Changing How We Experience What We Experience

Although psychotherapy has become the most established formal method of self-inquiry, it is obviously not the only way, nor is it necessarily the best way for any particular person at any particular time. Insights occur when one is ready for insight, and the moments and conditions that foster awareness are hardly restricted to the consulting room. Moreover, it may well be that, in addition to, or instead of, some adjustment within one's own personality, one requires a new look at relationships with the outside world and other people. For this purpose various kinds of group activities—formal group therapy, sensitivity training, encounter experiences—have been developed.

By its very nature individual psychotherapy is restricted to the relationship between the psychotherapist and the "patient." Not so the group experience. Here seven or eight people, each with his or her own personality and special set of experiences, can explore issues relevant to their interaction with one another—acceptance and rejection, competition, interdependency—under the direction of a trained leader.

"I just wasn't aware of the way I have of making disparaging remarks to anyone who showed any enthusiasm," recalled one group member. "Somehow other people's good spirits irritated me, and I was continually trying to puncture them. Sure, my wife had called me on this plenty of times, but I dismissed her criticism out of hand, figuring that she was anything but objective. But when the same observations came up in the group from total strangers who had no vested interest in saying it if it wasn't so, and especially when the leader played back the video tape he had of the encounter sessions, I had to stop and look at this reaction of mine more seriously and wonder what it was all about and how I could alter it."

Several years ago I participated in a two-day encounter session under the leadership of behavioral scientist Sherman Kingsbury. Seven other psychiatrists, colleagues, were there also. The most memorable part of the encounter weekend for me was an exercise to put us in touch with the importance of being able to be dependent and to trust.

For fifteen minutes, I was led about, blindfolded, by one of the other participants. He would take my hand and hold it out to touch the walls, pieces of furniture, lamps, glassware. At one point he took me down a steep staircase. All the while I was feeling anxious, wondering if I could really trust him not to guide me right into a closed door. Gradually, with the passage of time, my uneasiness evaporated and was replaced by a feeling of joy—and that is no exaggeration—at being able to have such confidence in another person. But that feeling, in turn, then gave way to some apprehension, and I thought, "Mustn't let yourself get too dependent or you'll be too vulnerable."

After the exercise, we shared the various ways we felt about what had happened. Some had handled it humorously or with thinly veiled sarcasm, joking back and forth with their guides. Others had remained uneasy throughout. One person had become aware of strong feelings of anger directed toward his guide, of "basically hating to be in that position with anyone."

What struck me about myself, at that point, was the fact that I had never really thought seriously about myself as being either independent or dependent, in spite of the fact that I had been practicing psychotherapy for a number of years and had been dealing with this very issue in person after person. For the first time I was forced to apply this insight to myself. And what was activated was a flood of recollections: being homesick the first year at camp; refusing in my late teens to listen to some pretty sound advice from my father, in order to prove that I was old enough to make my own decisions; keeping my own counsel, later on in life, when it would have served me well to ask for some advice; postponing the termination of a period of psychoanalysis after I felt that there was little more to be gained from it, because I had become dependent on the very routine of going to the analyst's office and lying on the couch four days a week at precisely nine-fifteen. My dependency needs were quite a bit stronger than I had cared to admit to myself, and I had been handling them most of the time by denying them, by trying to adhere to an unrealistic image of myself as a totally independent person. This insight, dealing as it did with a major underlying premise in my life, gradually and significantly changed the quality of my personal relationships; they have been closer and considerably more meaningful ever since.

Psychotherapist Frederick Perls was among the first to

recognize the tendency inherent in traditional psycho-analysis to fragment the personality and leave the individual with a series of isolated and disconnected insights. Through the process of dissecting motivations—the apparent from the real, the conscious from the unconscious—a person could readily end up feeling more pulled apart than before. And so Perls focused on the development of methods—rather dramatic at times—which would provide the person with a different route to awareness, one that would rapidly restore a sense of wholeness. The word *Gestalt* means "whole," and the methods which he and his associates developed focused on the issues of how one experiences oneself in a total way and how one perceives reality as a whole.

Gestalt techniques generally involve certain steps: the use of analogy, or likening yourself to an object; the analysis of the meaning of the intense feelings activated by the analogy; and, as in all such experiences, the reinforcement of the insight by suggestion. This use of analogy is an attempt to approach the insight from an unfamiliar direction, uncontaminated by language and preconceived labels. It is an effort to bypass the highly intellectual analysis of one's behavior so often unintentionally fostered by a more traditional "talk" approach to therapy, and thereby induce a more direct and genuine change in the way one perceives oneself and how one acts.

I once participated in a demonstration of this approach that was quite impressive. One woman in the group, when asked to close her eyes and experience herself as an inanimate object, thought for a moment and then came out with, "I feel like a piece of barbed wire. The wire extends through my whole body, into my arms and legs. It's jagged and rough." She was then asked to discuss how she felt about the experience, what it meant to her, and in the course of her comments she recognized a strong degree of resentment, concealed by an aloofness and distance she had usually maintained between herself and everyone else. "Don't get too close to me or you'll get hurt" was the message. She was then asked to close her eyes again and try to release herself from the barbed wire, to replace it with a substance and perception of herself which was less threatening. "I feel water running through my body and limbs, arms and legs, washing away the hatred," she reported. And with this shift in self-perception, she felt some degree of release and an ability to allow herself to be touched, literally and figuratively, by others in the group.

Another participant, a man, reported that he felt as if a steel rod were extended from the base of his skull to the tip of his spine. "I had no idea how much physical tension I had all through me until this exercise," he commented. "People used to tell me I was stiff, tense, always looking as if I were under pressure, but I never saw it myself, until now, and already I can feel some of it disappearing."

Observing this experience from a background of psychotherapy and psychoanalysis, I was particularly impressed by several things. First, it confirmed my own impression that most of us are often quite out of touch with our own feelings. And second, it suggested that if we could identify certain governing premises, underlying assumptions that control our own feelings and behavior, we could uncover them and change those that were based on perceptions no longer relevant, in this way accelerating the process of acquiring insight.

One such governing premise, for example, might be: "I am basically helpless, I cannot take care of myself, I need someone to take care of me." This kind of assumption would obviously not only delay the emergence of self-confidence in you if you were to act on it, but would also lead you to find yourself, again and again, in situations that either reaffirm your helplessness or at least allow you to feel confirmed in your sense of inadequacy. In your relationships with others, you would find yourself leaning on them in a precarious balance that inevitably would lead to being either controlled by them or rejected by them, if they found the burden of your dependency too great to carry. I have seen again and again, in individual therapy and group experiences, how efforts to recondition an individual toward a higher degree of self-reliance fail because they neglect to come to terms with the underlying, unrecognized premise that has influenced the person's behavior in so many ways, and often so surreptitiously, that dealing with one piece of specific behavior after another, bit by bit, usually produces no material change at all.

One of the troublesome aspects of the self-awareness and personal-improvement boom is the hope invested by the participants, and the promise often made by the proponents of a particular method, that this or that approach is the final word in the matter and that it will be some kind of definitive cure-all. If you learn to vent your angry feelings and be more self-assertive, if you can let out the essential primal scream, if you spend several thousand dollars and a week or two in St. Louis in a Masters and Johnson program, if you go to the West Coast, take off your clothes, confront yourself and others as you really are, everything will fall into place.

The one-shot experience, whatever it is, is seen not only as a cure-all for the epidemic of dissatisfaction with which we are all too familiar, but as a short, quick, dramatic, inexpensive experience to provide the insight to end all insights, to offer a formula that will suffice for a lifetime. The kinds of techniques have multiplied as quickly as the choices of cereal in the supermarket. And being suggestible, well-conditioned consumers, easily convinced of our "need" for any new product, we obtain some kind of emotional fulfillment from each experience. About the time that disappointment sets in, we are ready for the next approach that reaches the marketplace. For many, the compulsive search for awareness has become almost a way of life.

The fact is that any particular approach to insight—from psychoanalysis to transactional analysis to meditation—is decidedly limited in scope, regardless of its intrinsic value. Every person is sufficiently complex and life situations change so rapidly that no single focus, whether it is on how we react to those who would exploit us, how we perform in bed, how we handle anger, can be chosen as the primary and exclusive area worth investigating and trying to change. Not only that, but we run a high risk of ending up shakier than ever when we open ourselves up without the opportunity for synthesis to take place. We may become more aware, but nothing really gets resolved.

Several years ago, at the peak of the infectious en-counter-group fever, I visited a public school in New York where well-intentioned teachers were involved in holding weekly encounter sessions with twelve- and thirteen-year-old boys and girls. The purpose was to increase self-awareness and improve interpersonal relations. At the session at which I was present one boy talked about terrible conditions at home: his father away most of the time and when he was home, abusive to the mother and the children; his mother ill with diabetes and arthritis and barely able to care for the home and her family. He cried as he spoke, and one could feel his pain and helplessness only too clearly.

He was opening up, but nothing was being done to help him. I seriously questioned then, and still do, the wisdom of allowing this boy to confront himself with his feelings in front of twenty other youngsters who had no idea what to say to him and a discussion leader who had been trained to believe that opening up, by itself, was somehow curative. The teacher allowed the boy to go on without interruption, without offering any kind of helpful suggestion—no doubt having been taught a highly nondirective approach to self-revelation which was originally designed to deter leaders from intruding themselves too forcefully into counseling situations. Yet this boy was left hanging, with nothing resolved, without either the knowledge or the maturity to derive meaning from his experience. He had revealed himself intimately to his contemporaries, at an age when privacy is highly cherished, without anyone around afterward to help him make sense of, and cope with, a situation that he could do little to change.

The acquisition of insight takes place gradually over a lifetime, in such a variety of ways that any special technique to achieve it should be regarded as a catalyst rather than a solution. There are plenty of sources for new awareness in our experiences of everyday life. Making use of them requires an openness on our part and the ability to put them to work successfully. And this is precisely what mastery of the creative process permits us to do.

10
How to Become
More Creative

Keeping creativity alive is much easier than resurrecting it. If we are already used to approaching living with imagination, we will tend to do so automatically in the face of new stresses. If we are not, we shall then, like a child learning letters, have to cultivate our creative ability slowly, haltingly, grasping some of the basic principles involved and using them—in a word, practicing.

The best way to begin is to think of yourself as creative. And this is made easier by separating yourself from the trappings of the particular role you have in life: housewife, mother, business executive, mechanic, grandfather, student. Even if we are not fully aware of it, we identify with the part we play in life. The tighter the straitjacket of "I am what I do," the more difficult it is to deal with any new set of circumstances. Each role carries expectations with it that will keep getting in the way. The more my white physician's coat invades and defines my personality, the less capable I will be of considering original solutions to problems that arise, whether personal or professional.

Do clothes reflect the person? Can you actually become more creative by changing the way you dress? To the extent that what you wear reflects you, the answer is yes. Of course, to change what you wear is only a technique to stimulate changing your self-image, reducing the impact of the conformist artifacts that are counterproductive to creativity. It is the inner changes that count; it is the separation of your sense of identity from the responsibilities you have that will free you to entertain unexpected and singularly original ideas. The "I am I" perception of yourself has a uniqueness that the "I am what I do" self-image can never have. The "I am I" perception can liberate spontaneity, making you more open to fresh concepts as well as to your own inner, unconscious resources.

Our environment affects our creativity. There are often special circumstances under which we are more likely to think in a creative way. Everyone can ask: Under what conditions am I most likely to gain new insights? In quiet and relaxation? At home or away from home? When there is something to increase my general level of tension? Are there people around me who turn my imagination on? Are there people around me who seriously interfere with my doing any original thinking? Am I better off trying to do it alone? Do I need a certain amount of security, economic or emotional, in work, in my personal life, to feel free to think?

Characteristics of the Creative Person

A mass of information about the creative process has emerged from the extensive research of recent years. From this information we can get quite a clear picture of what characteristics belong to the creative person, and we can learn some very specific principles to get our own creativity going.

Creative people are flexible. They are also stable. They are in rather good balance, within themselves, in their relationships with the world. They can use their minds to evaluate and judge, can rely on their intuition to arrive at insights that originate in their unconscious, can recover from periods when their stability is disrupted. They have little resemblance to the myth that assumes the creative person to be unstable or at least mildly neurotic. Moreover, the possession of an unusual talent, however striking, does not in and of itself make for a personality that is creative. Many famous artists are highly creative in special areas, but their adaptation to life in general is often anything but creative.

Creative people also possess a high degree of self-sufficiency; they are by no means without attachments, but their need to depend is not so strong or misdirected that it short-circuits their creative energy. They can remain free of the confusion and standards of the society around them. Although, being human, they are not without need for approval, they do not need it so much that they must give up their originality to gain it.

Their concern for the opinion of others and for certain social norms is far more evident in their thinking than in their behavior. They may have a different vision of things, but there is no evidence to support the commonly held assumption that they actively, antagonistically, oppose the current order of things in a categorical rebelliousness.

Creative individuals are gifted with a unique ability to

tolerate ambiguity, not only in work but in personal life. There is no way, for example, that a man or woman can enter marriage in contemporary society, in view of the high divorce rate, without mixed feelings of commitment and uncertainty. There is no way that men can reconsider the nature of masculinity or women the essentials of femininity without going through a period of considerable uneasiness as they sift the germane from the superficial, abandoning what they once thought to be a prerogative or fundamental characteristic of their sex and moving hesitantly, uncomfortably, and with some risk toward a new concept of themselves, one which may itself become unraveled with time and change.

Jung described four basic types of people according to their predominant mode of perception—that is, how each views and responds to any stimuli arising from themselves or their outer world. His four types were the *thinking*, the *feeling*, the *sensate*, and the *intuitive*. He defined the thinking type as the individual who logically structures, analyzes, and synthesizes information by means of conceptual generalizations. The feeling type emphasizes values and human relationships. The person who operates primarily through sensation perceives external reality and adapts to it by way of the senses: this is the pragmatist. The intuitive type perceives primarily along nonconscious routes, frequently bypassing ordinary logic, and is rapidly in touch with his or her own unconscious.

Everyone is a mixture of these types but usually with one form of perception dominant. It is the intuitive mode of perception, above all, that appears to be most essential to creativity. The presence of other modes of perception in a prominent degree may determine how effectively the creative ideas are developed and applied and to what end they may be put.

Intuition is quite different from impulsiveness or whim. It does not mean offending common sense. There is nothing magical about it, although it often seems irrational to those who are either unfamiliar with it, see it only in others, or have not learned to trust their own intuition. It is the added ingredient in decision making, after the facts and figures have been reasonably analyzed, that presses us to move in one direction or another.

If intuitiveness is accompanied by a considerable degree of the thinking type of perception, the individual may become engaged in highly productive scientific work. If feeling accompanies intuition, the individual's values and interpersonal relationships will receive special emphasis. If the sensate form is prominent in the combination, the result may be quite profitable from an economic point of view. As an investment counselor put it, "We add up facts and figures about corporate profits and sales trends and competition and economic shifts. But when the time for decision making comes, whether to invest or not, I experience a sense of rightness or wrongness about the decision which is compelling, which does not always follow the course dictated by the accumulation of facts, but which, if followed, is more often successful than not, and if ignored, has proved to be disastrous."

Another common characteristic of the creative personality is a wide range of interests and with these a high level of curiosity. Creative individuals are seldom afraid to explore unfamiliar things, to acknowledge themselves dilettantes—in the original sense of the word, before it implied a frivolous superficiality of interest and indicated, instead, someone who cultivated a branch of knowledge as a pastime without pursuing it professionally. At the same time, creative people have the energy and discipline to see through to completion the tasks they believe worth doing.

"The only success which is ours to command," said Justice Oliver Wendell Holmes, "is to bring to our work a mighty heart." Passion, commitment, energy, and courage are part of the creative personality. These qualities add up to a high level of energy with a strong sense of purpose and direction that reflects the creative person's innate urge to live. That energy is free, some of the time in most creative people, much of the time in a select few, to channel itself spontaneously toward constructive purposes with a sense of commitment. This drive has a genuineness to it which clearly distinguishes it from both the pressured style of the compulsive individual and the frantic enthusiasm of the manic.

The pathological often sheds light on the commonplace. As a young doctor in charge of a research unit in which I was investigating biochemical factors in depression, and hence in an area where a number of depressed patients were located, I thought it might be helpful to introduce a somewhat hypomanic patient to the group. The purpose was to add a touch of cheerfulness and humor into an otherwise gloomy and oppressive environment. The result was quite the opposite. The depressed patients fled the scene, retreating to their rooms, and what little sense of community there had been vanished within a day. What I had underestimated was the extent to which the seemingly energetic and hopeful manic patient was actually hostile, disruptive, domineering, and disturbing, and how his flow of ideas, rather than being creative, was actually bombastic, subtly grandiose, certainly egocentric in the extreme, and quite lacking in any meaningful interaction with the world around him.

The enthusiasm of the creative person may or may not be visible, but it is quite a different kind of involvement from the hyperactivity with which it is often confused.

Principles of Creative Thinking

The results of extensive research on creativity provide not only a profile of the creative personality but a set of specific principles that we can use to get our own creativity going.

DEFERRED JUDGMENT. One such principle is the rule of deferred judgment. Postponing an evaluation of our own ideas or those of others as they are being conjured up and put into words is essential but not easy. Normally we weigh our ideas, good or bad, useful or senseless, possible or ridiculous, acceptable or terrible, at the moment they occur to us. Withholding judgment in the search for unexpected solutions allows for a greater flow of ideas from which, eventually, will come the really original ones. Psychologist Sidney Parnes has called this the principle of extended effort. It seems to loosen the attachment to pre-existing concepts and perceptions that effectively block new and unfamiliar ones.

The way we perceive ourselves or reality is strongly influenced by our past experience. Inevitably, new information is first seen as it relates to the familiar. If it corresponds to what we already know, it is generally acceptable. The technique of deferred judgment is designed precisely for the purpose of bypassing such fixed assumptions. It also helps us refrain from logical and analytic thought processes for a while, thus fostering spontaneity and increasing the total flow of ideas.

QUANTITY LEADS TO QUALITY. Increasing the total flow of ideas is another essential part of the creative process. The more suggestions we can come up with in response to a given problem or opportunity, the more likely we are to discover new and meaningful answers. Whether we are dealing with a profound problem in research or such a mundane issue as how to spend the coming weekend, the very first idea we arrive at is seldom new. It is more likely to be stamped indelibly with the mark of what we already know about the problem we are exploring. It is more likely to resemble what we did last weekend or the weekend before.

Both deferring judgment and recognizing that quantity leads to quality put us in close contact with unconscious sources of creativity. There is a remarkable resemblance between the techniques that psychologists have developed to stimulate creative thinking and the process of free association. In fact, the concept of free association developed by Freud may have been partially stimulated by a set of principles already set forth by the German journalist Ludwig Börne to enhance creative thinking. In his biography of Freud, Ernest Jones mentions that Freud was familiar with an essay by Börne entitled "The Art of Becoming an Original Writer in Three Days," written in 1823. Börne wrote:

Here follows the practical prescription I promised. Take a few sheets of paper and for three days in succession write down, without any falsification or hypocrisy, everything that comes into your head. Write what you think of yourself, of your women, of the Turkish war, of Goethe, of the Fonk criminal case, of the Last Judgment, of those senior to you in authority—and when the three days are over you will be amazed at what novel and startling thoughts have welled up in you.

REDEFINING THE PROBLEM. An extremely useful method of stimulating original thinking is to redefine the problem that you are trying to solve. Find new words to describe it. Ask questions in a different way. As long as a particular issues is stated in a certain way—"Should I start thinking about a divorce?" or "Should I quit this job and find another?"—it may defy resolution for months, years, even forever. Restating the problem in a different way can be the first step toward discovering the solution. Instead of asking "Should I get a divorce?" you might ask: "What have my expectations of marriage been? What are they now—still the same? Does it make more sense to be on my own?" Similarly, you might question: "To what degree does the work I am doing reflect my basic interests and use my abilities fully?" or "How much money do I really need to earn?" Or again, "How do I want to spend the hours of the day, doing what kind of tasks, finding what kind of satisfactions, being with what kind of people?" Then, from a long list of answers to such questions, try to narrow the possibilities down to those few that make sense and could be implemented.

I can recall going through just that process some years

ago. It did not result in a change in the actual work I was doing, but, by redefining the issues, I discovered a new way to experience my work. As many of us do, I had for years segmented my life into compartments; in my case, teaching, research, and treating patients were work activities in contrast to being with my family and friends and pursuing outside interests. Work and play—work was assumed to be difficult and tiring and play enjoyable. I began to rethink this matter. To the question "How do I like spending my days?" I answered, to myself, "With people." I soon realized that I genuinely enjoyed being with my patients as people and that to distinguish between the time spent with them and the time spent with friends was an artificial construct. In some instances I recognized that I liked and respected many of my patients far more than any of my acquaintances.

DISTANCING. The way we think things are is what keeps us from seeing how they might be, and not infrequently even how they really are. Distancing affords a clearer view. If you walk out of a forest and up a nearby hill, the nature of the woods at once becomes obvious. Putting some space between ourselves and our problems often stimulates new solutions. There are various ways—geographic distancing, a vacation, for example; time distancing, putting the problem aside for a while to let it simmer; mental distancing, accomplished, by some, through meditation—to clear the head and make room for new concepts to enter afterward. When we are confronted with a problem, we tend to think that the best approach is to attack it head on or go over and over it until it yields. By doing so, we often only reinforce the very obstacles that keep us from seeing answers.

Another form of distancing is humor. Through humor we put space between ourselves and something that we might find frightening or otherwise upsetting. It can trigger movement through an impasse, and because it allows us to be instantly in touch with ideas we might ordinarily find incongruous and incompatible, humor acts as a catalyst to stimulate unthought-of and unexpected possibilities. Quite often in therapy I use absurd juxtapositions and images to stimulate laughter, when it is appropriate and not done at the patient's expense or my own.

Specific methods to activate creativity are very useful, especially while we are learning. But they should not be confused with the cultivation over a period of time of a fundamental attitude toward living that is itself inherently creative. Tennyson wrote in "Ulysses":

> Yet all experience is an arch wherethro'
> Gleams that untravell'd world, whose margin fades
> For ever and for ever when I move.

Ultimately such a frame of mind requires a major shift in the way we see ourselves and the world around us. Creativity may be natural to children, but keeping that attitude alive through periods of barrenness or depression depends largely on our intentional efforts to sustain it. In doing so, we must often work against the nature of education and the culture in which we live, which conspire to block these efforts.

For most of us, in our work, in our personal lives, there are usually a few central issues, recurring again and again, that cause us the most anguish. Year in and year out we complain about working conditions. We argue with our husbands and wives about the same things—sex, money, in-laws. We try desperately but in vain to get the other person to agree with our point of view. Even when we are free to do otherwise, the herd instinct presses us to go where everyone else is going, to live where everyone else lives, and to take a vacation where everyone else does, even if it means that we will have to pay twice as much money for the privilege of doing so and spend hours on throughways soaked with carbon monoxide. "For want of an effective concept of humanity," wrote Antoine de Saint-Exupéry, "we have been slipping gradually towards the ant-hill, whose definition is the mere sum of the individuals it contains."

One of the very first steps to becoming more creative is the willingness to leave the main thoroughfare from time to time and explore some of the back roads and lanes, to be different, to be singular. The Greeks believed that a man's destiny lay in his character. Now, more than ever, we have the means to decipher our characters, drawing from our conclusions that which makes each of us unique. This willingness to be individual and to cultivate an open mind and spirit, letting go of unworkable premises to find better ones, is what prepares us to improve the quality of our lives at best, and, at the very least, to survive.

11
A Total More Than
the Sum of Its Parts

More often than not, original thinking is best done in solitude. At certain times one can only think things through
and reach new conclusions alone. However, the people
around us seriously influence the way we live and work in
that they help to establish either an environment in which
creativity can flourish or one in which it may only smolder
or even die. Others can contribute to our creativity by simply letting us be by ourselves at times without making us
feel guilty about it.

Beyond this, however, the quality of our interaction
with others can reinforce our own creativeness, so that the
total effect may be much greater than what any one of us
might accomplish alone. There are many times and many
conditions when the imagination of one person is not
enough to bring about a new solution, when the combined
talents and knowledge of a number of people are essential
for a creative result.

This is true in business, for example. "Today's success

comes from yesterday's creativeness," writes management consultant Antony Jay in *Management and Machiavelli*. Management, he points out, even at the moment of concerning itself with the more mechanical aspects of carrying out a well-defined task, "should be concerned about tomorrow's success . . . and tomorrow's success comes from today's creativeness." In successful business organizations, the pooling of knowledge and abilities is well balanced. It would make no sense to start a new company with a product to sell unless the core group of people contained members who understood or were experienced in selling. Otherwise, although the group might put together a unique and highly useful product, the company would never be able to survive economically because no one knew enough about marketing it. The knowledge base must be there in order for any group to accomplish its purpose. Obvious as this may seem, it is a rule that is broken again and again in the selection of people to do a particular job.

A creative group has distinct advantages over the individual working in isolation. To begin with, the input of knowledge and experience is increased, not just arithmetically but geometrically. Imagine each person as a circle. Then picture these circles intersecting, the lines of each crossing the others in such a way that, while there is a central area of common talent and purpose, there is also within each circle a large area which is separate and represents the unique qualities and particular backgrounds of each member of the group that can be introduced into the creative process as sources of ideas, stimulation, and, eventually, evaluations and conclusions.

Whether we consider it consciously or not, each of us

belongs to certain groups, which may be intentionally formed or just happen. A family is a group, and it exerts its influence on how its members function long after they cease to live under the same roof. Larger groups may be ethnic, religious, political, economic. There are invisible groups out of the past—teachers, friends, students— who have in one way or another stimulated our thinking and often contributed substantially to our own originality. There are the obvious groups—the committees we belong to, the organizations we work in, the clubs we join.

Groups form within groups, and as the size of organizations grows and the sense of community correspondingly diminishes, subgroups assume greater strength and meaning. They have their own life cycle. They are born; they mature; they die. They may constitute an environment in which originality flourishes, or they may be counterproductive to any creativity at all. They may also possess a creative energy of their own that arises spontaneously or is set in motion for a particular purpose.

The Creative Group in Action

Whether a group is put together by selection or happenstance, there are certain rules to follow if the members wish to work toward original solutions or carry out a course of action.

Some years ago I decided to experiment with the problem of increasing the creative abilities of groups to deal with particular tasks. One of the groups that I met was made up of highly intelligent, well-motivated members of a college faculty. They had been struggling for over a year to come to some sort of agreement about a new curriculum structure. The group consisted of fourteen department heads. We spent a weekend working together and, essentially, playing games.

Saturday morning I asked them to break into two subgroups of seven each to talk about the controversial curriculum. As before, they made no progress, becoming rapidly involved in stalemates, adamant positions, misunderstandings. That afternoon I asked them to carry out an exercise—to depart from the theme of the curriculum and work together to solve a different problem. They must design a business or activity of some kind by which they could earn a living. It could not have anything to do with teaching, but, it must be an enterprise that involved all of them in common and one for which their own backgrounds and experiences could somehow have prepared them. Most important, they must approach the exercise as a game.

The *gamelike quality*—the playfulness—of the experience was emphasized. Research and experiments in creativity have demonstrated that the concept of play, by supplying both freedom and rules, establishes a condition in which creative ideas can emerge in a group. There are set limits that make the situation nonthreatening and without serious consequences. Without play—or humor, which is a part of play—there is a sense of danger that blocks the expression of unusual or different thoughts as well as the willingness to take innovative risks.

The basic principles of the creative group process, which have been carefully worked out by behavioral scientists who have studied this process for years, became immediately and forcefully apparent to the college faculty members. As in the case of individual creativity, it is important to generate as many different ideas as possible—a process called brainstorming—and at the same time to defer passing judgment on these ideas until much later. The faculty members began to see, painfully, how quickly they would jump into the discussion to criticize, with such comments as "That won't work" or "Nobody will buy that kind of service" or "It's already been done." Until instructed to do so, they also failed to assess the talent and experience of each member of the group before making suggestions about the problem. Gradually they discovered, to their surprise, that among one subgroup of seven, one person was an accomplished writer, another had had considerable experience in public relations on behalf of community activities with which he had been involved, a third had a good head for figures, a fourth was an excellent chef, a fifth had been trained as an accountant before going into teaching as a career, a sixth had been a professional athlete, and the seventh had had a rather successful business of his own for several years before he realized that the pressures of the business world were not to his liking and decided to move into the academic world.

As the group began working with this information—the members forcing themselves to withhold the evaluations that flashed through their minds with each new idea presented—they were again reminded to look on what they were doing as simply a game, not as if there would be serious consequences if they did not produce a solution, or as if their futures were on the line. The point was to let go, to keep an element of humor going, and most of all to enjoy what they were trying to do together.

This reminder enabled them to start moving on the project with renewed enthusiasm. They were quite willing to consider that the solution they sought might be quite an unexpected one. "Running a restaurant," "publishing a magazine for sportsmen," "opening a resort hotel in the Caribbean," and a dozen other possibilities were suggested before they finally settled for opening a health spa for tired and harassed executives, along the lines of Maine Chance for women, but coeducational. And as they moved toward a conclusion, considering the various aspects of the venture—whether they really had the ability to handle it, whether they could raise the money to begin it, whether they could entice clients to come; assigning roles and responsibilities, roughly estimating what the charges should be and what they would offer for the price, planning how they would advertise it—they moved together in a harmony and unity they had never experienced in the years they had been associated with one another at the college.

The next day the faculty members were asked to return to the subject of the curriculum to see whether what they had learned the previous day would affect their ability to deal with that impasse. Step by step, they began to wade through the old biases and assumptions and obstacles, seeing the substantial difference between the game they had played and the serious business at hand. But there was now a major difference in their approach: although they were not by any means able to resolve completely the many issues involved, they were able to distinguish between legitimate areas of conflict and primarily interpersonal oppositions and clashes.

It is the quality of the interpersonal relationships that either catalyzes or cripples the creative energies of any group. The tendency to personalize is an example. There is a considerable difference between attacking a person and going after a point. And there is a substantial difference between hearing a negative comment on your opinion as a stimulus to rethink or clarify and hearing it as a hurtful, compromising, challenging put-down.

Most people working in groups fall into this kind of trap. Either the disagreements become colored by personal aspersions—whether explicitly stated or implied by a tone of voice that makes it sound as if what had just been said was ridiculous or reflective of poor judgment and unsound mind—or there is virtually total silence, because everyone is fearful either of being attacked or of being misread as attacking, and so does not offer anything of substance to press the creative process forward.

Competition, whether open and fierce or subtle and concealed, is often the basis for of such impasses. A good point made by someone else is regarded as something taken away from oneself. To talk freely is to run the risk of opening oneself to criticism later on by someone who uses what has been said as a weapon in a manipulative play for power or position. Throughout the creative process the members of the group must retain, as much as they can, a sense of being on the same side, working toward the same end, and—easy to say, so difficult to implement—an atmosphere of mutual trust.

The spoken word, of course, is only one medium of communication. Without the use of words, ideas and feelings are regularly being channeled among the members of any group. A glance, a smile, restless movements of the legs, a yawn, a raised eyebrow, a deep sigh, sitting forward in one's chair to listen more intently—these are only some of the more obvious clues which people in groups give to one another to signify acceptance or rejection of what one person is contributing, and of the person himself. Being human, we are turned on by acceptance and rapidly obliterated by rejection, and the lower the threshold for rejection is, the harder it will be to feel free to express oneself.

And there is the other side of the coin: conscientiousness has become so overly democratized that we are often just as much afraid of rejecting as of being rejected and in consequence fail to put limits on the behavior of others in the group, thus giving some members the liberty to destroy the creative process by dominating or controlling the group to further their own goals or needs.

A group that is effectively engaged in the creative process has a movement. It is a movement that could almost be recorded on tape as the sounds of voices brushing against one another, the rhythm of periodic silences, the ebb and flow of volume, and sudden bursts of energy when all the voices sound at once. Every group has a characteristic motion of its own. Once, for fun and as an experiment, I collected a number of tapes of various types of conferences and played each of them on a recorder at high speed, listening not so much for content as for the flow of the sound. Even at high speed, unproductive groups sounded slow, sluggish, monotonous, uninspiring, with seemingly interminable pauses between voices. In other groups, a rapid, staccato, piercing, colliding pattern of voices overriding one another developed when the participants became so wound up that no structure could be maintained, and no matter what ideas were produced, the outcome could only be chaotic. Try, on some occasion, to remove the words from what you are saying, listen to the basic sound of it, and consider.

Any group that wishes to improve its level of creativity can take encouragement from the fact that practice makes a difference. As psychologist Sidney Parnes reported:

> The practice element seems to be crucial in cultivating creative behavior. . . . Creativity development programs will typically provide a good deal of practice in deferring judgment, in playing with ideas and forcing new relationships, in alternating between involvement with and detachment from the problem. Striking evidence of the value of such practice was provided by a comparative study of novices and those experienced in the use of deferred judgment. . . . Even though both groups were given the intellectual set of deferring judgment, relating freely, striving for quantity of alternatives, the experienced subjects . . . out-produced the novices . . . approximately two to one on both quantity and quality of ideas in solution to a problem.

The chief research in the principles of group creativity has been done by experimental psychologists at such institutions as the Center for Creative Studies in Buffalo, New York, and at Massachusetts Institute of Technology in Cambridge. Their work has focused primarily on two issues: the use of group dynamics to heighten the creative abilities of each member in the group, and practice and experience in the creative process, such as deferred judgment and brainstorming, to enhance the innovative output of the whole group working together. The most effective size for such a group has proved to be seven or eight members.

Anticreative Forces

Such small groups, unfortunately, live and work within larger social structures known as institutions. However creative the small group may be, it is at the institutional level that real trouble begins.

Even a large organization began somewhere, usually with an innovative idea: an instrument that copies documents hundreds at a time; a new way to market a concept to the public; a plan to bring peace to a section of the world previously torn apart by war; a fresh approach to a social problem such as public health or unemployment. At the beginning the creative force is not hard to identify.

The challenge comes when an organization has established itself and achieved a certain degree of success. Then it is confronted with a new kind of stress, one which most organizations cannot handle. Can the original purpose be sustained and built upon constructively? Are there new purposes that the organization can serve? Or must it redefine itself, and in so doing ask whether it has any justification at all for its continued existence? Has it outlived its usefulness and so should cease to exist in order that the cumulative talents of its members may be released to form new organizations that meet new needs?

I am by no means alone in the belief that bureaucracy is a major enemy of creativity. In the field of drug-abuse prevention, for example, hundreds of millions of dollars were spent in an attempt to warn teenagers in classrooms of the dangers of using drugs. The money was often dis-

tributed without regard to either the originality or the wisdom of any particular approach. It was as if a helicopter
had flown over the roofs and playgrounds of a thousand
schools and dropped a shower of hundred-dollar bills into
the area, in the hope that as a result fewer youngsters
would become involved in the drug scene. What was
clearly and repeatedly lacking was any creative forethought
or any effort to set up model programs which could be
tested and retested on smaller scales and then applied with
efficiency on a broader scale. As a necessary corollary, the
thousands of people who had become a part of the prevention programs soon saw a need to figure out ways of insuring their continued employment. Literally within weeks of
being hired, they were extensively concerned with how to
convince the state or national governments to prolong
their budgets beyond the established time period.

Immobilization and a serious loss of integrity are the
natural consequences of bureaucracy. "To keep things
under control," wrote Alan Watts, "it proliferates laws of
ever-increasing complexity and unintelligibility, and
hinders productive work by demanding so much account-
ing on paper that the record of what has been done becomes more important than what has actually been done."
Nearly two thousand years before Christ, Watts points out,
the Emperor Han Kao Tsu, founder of the Han dynasty,
which endured for four hundred years, abolished all the
repressive laws of the former government and proclaimed
that "hereafter only three simple laws shall prevail:
namely, that manslaughter shall be punished by death,
and that assault and theft shall be justly punished according to the facts of each case."

Though simplification and a reduction in complex controls clearly increase the productivity of most organizations and set the stage for innovation, there must obviously be a sufficient degree of structure to permit routine activities to be carried out with dispatch. A system of checks and balances is necessary to reduce the possibility of fraud. But when regulations replace concern with motivation and morale, the organization, whatever its nature and purpose, is in serious difficulty.

Most of the groups to which we belong and with which we identify exist within the shadow of these larger systems. And it is the character of these smaller groups that we are in the best position to influence. This is especially true of that group we call the family, where the prevailing attitudes, modes of communication, and values will determine whether the creativity of its members will be stimulated or suppressed, and whether, as a whole, the family will move toward its objectives and resolve conflicts in a creative manner.

12
Creativity
in the Family

The trouble with marriage today is that it is no longer sustained by the external supports that once protected it. Men and women now live longer, expect more, and focus critically on the quality of the relationship that exists between them. Never has creativity been so essential to the success of family life.

Reconciliation: An Exercise in Creativity

Perhaps the most serious and destructive problem in modern family life is the inability to achieve reconciliations. The term reconciliation, unfortunately, has acquired misleading legal overtones. It implies that a couple have separated and are considering a divorce, and that because of a change of heart or some family or professional pressure they have decided to try once again. In a wider sense, reconciliation should be thought of as the restoration of contact and communication between two people after any experience—an argument, a misunderstanding—has disrupted those aspects of the relationship.

Advocates of free speech and healthy emotional exchanges recommend that husbands and wives be able to get angry and to express anger when they feel it, instead of suppressing it for days, weeks, months. There is much to be said for this point of view, but "making up," the second step that such a suggestion entails—restoring equilibrium and closeness after this kind of explosion—is rarely dealt with adequately. Forgiving is confused with forgetting, and so any reference indicating recollection of an episode that disturbed the relationship is resentfully interpreted as unreasonable and unforgiving.

Reconciliation in its true sense involves letting go of the hurt without necessarily forgetting the experience itself. As such, it is a rather complex psychological process involving the separation of feelings from memory, a reconsideration of the event in the light of the total perspective of the relationship. An occasional failure of contact in an otherwise close and healthy relationship is one thing; breaks that outweigh periods of harmony in frequency and duration are quite another. Reconciliation also involves a deepening of insight. Was the issue that triggered the anger or hurt the true issue or simply the wrong feeling directed toward the wrong person at the wrong time? Is there some other and more serious issue behind the one which set off the quarrel?

If forgiveness involves a reconsideration, then it is by definition a creative experience, one which forces a new point of view on the relationship. "Love," as one character in Erich Segal's novel *Love Story*, says, "means never having to say you're sorry." Nothing could be further from the truth. Apologizing is important. But to be meaningful it must imply genuine regret at having hurt the other person, some degree of insight into what has happened, and the ability and willingness to rethink the pressures that provoked the blow-up in the first place.

The alternative, of course, is to walk away. This is difficult in a tightly structured society but remarkably easy in one such as ours, where the values determining not only behavior but expectations of behavior are so blurred that abruptly walking away from something or walking out on someone is considered perfectly rational, or at worst mildly irresponsible.

The ability to become reconciled in the psychological sense, after a breach has occurred, is only one example of the way the creative process can operate within a close relationship, in marriage or elsewhere. This process includes the examination of the underlying conflict that may have set the stage for the break in closeness and communication. Is it a problem of compatibility? Carl Jung speaks of compatibility between people as being intimately related to perception. And psychologist Robert McCully has said, "One of the most common clinical situations in which difficulty in communication derives from different perceptual modes is the marital dilemma in which opposite [perceptual] types frequently misunderstand each other's judgments and motivations."

The need for privacy is a good example of such misunderstanding. What distinguishes Jung's extravert (popularly misinterpreted, in terms of a behavioral pattern, as the outgoing, backslapping party-goer) is in fact a different mode of perception; extraverts do tend to shun solitude but do so because they define their world through perception of the external world, through outer objects and events, through human relationships. They tend to want to be with others, depend more heavily on others' opinions for their own sense of identity, and quickly tire of reflective pursuits. By contrast, introverts rely primarily on sorting and sifting perceptions through inner reactions and images; thus they are happier when left to their own devices, free from the pressure to adapt to external conditions. They are more private people.

The failure of a somewhat extraverted husband to comprehend his wife's introverted need for private time—misinterpreting it, perhaps, as a form of rejection—can give rise to serious conflict. Any need she may have to be alone, reading, or whatever, may be interpreted by him as not wanting to be with him. Hurt and perhaps angry, he may withdraw in retaliation or periodically reach out to disturb her solitude. The relationship cannot remain alive unless both realize this difference and its sources and correct their perceptions of it so as to stop assuming that a particular piece of behavior, such as talking or not talking, means the same thing to both. Acquiring this insight is an exercise in empathy. It involves being able to let go of the assumption that the world is as I perceive it and grasp the concept that, however close and compatible people may be in general, there are bound to be significant differences in perception between them. The ability to imagine how someone else feels and to take it into account is a good example of creativity at work; it requires looking at a familiar thing in a new and unexpected way.

When people resemble each other, there is a built-in compatibility. When they do not, the diversity must be understood and accepted—and appreciated—if the relationship is to work.

Insight as a Barometer

There are even more important implications for marriage that arise from the consideration of creativity and its companion, insight. If you have ever lived in close quarters emotionally with a person lacking in insight, you know how persistently frustrating the experience can be. No amount of discussion, no repeated efforts at clarification, no constructive suggestions seem to make even a minor dent on the surface of a closed mind. The psychiatrist Wilhelm Reich gave the name "armor" to those character traits which people develop to protect themselves against insight. And armor they are. One of the first questions that occurs to a psychiatrist evaluating a depressed individual or to a physician getting a reading of high blood pressure is, or should be, whether this patient is living with someone who has little or no insight.

Marriage counselors use a rough estimate of the level of insight as a barometer to determine the chances of success in any effort to bring about reconciliation or some improvement in the quality of a marriage. They want to see not only whether any insight is there but if it is not, how much time and energy might be required to develop it. If a person who lacks insight is potentially creative, he or she will at least be open to acquiring this quality, since flexibility is an important component of creativity.

Decision making in marriage quickly shows whether or not the creative process is being used.

"We solved our difficulties in only one way—by doing it his way," said one woman. "I thought that was what I should do as a wife. And in the course of forfeiting my own ideas again and again, I accumulated layers of resentment which, at the same time, managed to wreck my sense of self-esteem, too."

Or again, as a husband described it, "Decision making was a trade-off in our house. We could as well have kept a list, the things she wanted to do that I did reluctantly, the things I wanted to do that she did with equal reluctance. And don't think we didn't both keep track of each compromise—with arithmetical precision."

There is always a give-and-take in close relationships, but in a creative environment it is without the kind of tightness and compulsiveness that leaves everyone gasping for air. Rather, as with the resolution of conflict, the choice of direction—whether in something as minor as how to spend a holiday or something of such major consequence as where to live or how to spend retirement years—entails a process quite similar to that described by the psychologists exploring creativity. Many ideas are produced. They are considered without critical judgment for a while. They are allowed to simmer, sitting, as it were, on the back burner. Eventually they crystallize, and concrete steps are taken to explore how practical they are. And, most important, there is a spirit of cooperation that generates new and better options and makes the resolution, when it is reached, one that is basically gratifying for both partners.

Creativity and Sex

The passionate, erotic, purely sensual quality of the sexual experience is not long-lived. For many men and women, the newness of the experience heightens the sexual tension, especially when a factor that elevates the anxiety level, such as illicitness or a fear of "being caught," is present. But, as is well known, over a period of time this tension subsides. What, then, can keep sexual fulfillment between two people alive over a period of years? Love, caring? This is part of it, as the more essentially erotic drives combine with sensitivity, respect, wanting to give pleasure as much as to receive it. Compatibility? Certainly the more compatibility—when the two people perceive life similarly, though with sufficient differences to permit diversity—the more harmonious a relationship will be and the longer sexual interest will last. The most common cause of loss of sexual interest is not lack of know-how, nor is it boredom. It is the accumulation of unresolved resentments and misunderstandings, frequently originating in differing modes of perception and conflicting value systems, and occurring in an atmosphere which discourages the free and direct expression of ideas and feelings. Under such circumstances, a rift can become wider and wider until it may actually defy healing altogether.

Husbands and wives are now encouraged to talk with each other about their sexual life together. They are also encouraged to discuss their sexual experiences in general, although, especially when infidelity is involved, this is more likely to be an exercise in tactlessness and poor judgment than an indication of good communication. There is no doubt, however, that greater freedom to put into words what you feel about sex, for your own benefit as well as to better the understanding of the other person, is important. Such communication will help clarify how you actually perceive the sexual experience and so may lead to a more creative approach to sex. A better sex life and a more imaginative one, stemming from such mutual understanding, is quite different from pure diversity for its own sake or assuming various positions suggested by some handbook or other.

Varying conditions can enhance sexual fulfillment, to be sure. Under what conditions are you more likely to be sexually aroused? On a vacation? After an evening of intimacy, having had dinner together, talking? On the spur of the moment? In the daytime? When there is a reasonable amount of privacy? When the pressures and strains of the day have been minimal? These are questions which every book on sex raises, but the extent to which people can put the answers into practice, in a novel and enjoyable way, clearly depends on their flexibility and ability to learn.

Creativity is also involved in keeping sex alive in a more fundamental way. A common turning point in the sex life of a married couple is the birth of the first child. The husband is now a father, the wife a mother. Inevitably, a conflict arises, the resolution of which demands the ability to balance apparently contradictory concepts—in this case, the problem of self-image. While there are certainly exceptions, the concepts of being a parent and also having an active and sensual sexual life tend to be contradictory, consciously or unconsciously, for most people. The increase in sexual drive observed in women nearing forty quite possibly takes place not only for biological reasons and in order to reassure themselves about their sexual attractiveness, but because, now that their children are teenagers, or even grown up and with sexual lives of their own, they have time and freedom to reconsider themselves as women, apart from their role as mothers, and so remove a major obstacle to thinking of themselves sexually.

One way to keep sex alive in marriage is to be able to move freely from one role to another, even though these roles seem to conflict. Better yet is to avoid thinking of them as roles at all, but rather for both men and women to search for a unifying identity that allows them to be themselves in a variety of circumstances and to carry out a variety of tasks. In this way, the impact of preset assumptions on individual expectations can be diminished, lessening the need for a couple to conform to established patterns of behavior that may be unsuitable for them.

The Family Atmosphere

The quality of the relationship between husband and wife will decide the extent to which either can fulfill his or her creative potential. This, in turn, sets the stage for the kind of family life they will have.

Family life is the breeding ground for creativity or for the lack of it. One of the characteristics of the creative person is the ability to be in touch with his or her own feelings and to direct their expression into appropriate chanels. This is learned by growing up in a family milieu that encourages a balance between individuality and realistic limits.

Unfortunately the development of such a balance, essential for creativity, is often blocked. Rather than becoming creative, "the child is led to dissociate from his emotions and from his feelings of effectiveness," says psychiatrist Peter Hogan, "and to adopt the view of reality espoused by others. For the parental figures, the goal (which may be quite unconscious) is to 'train' the child; in brief, to keep him amenable to their control." The result of this process is that the children grow up to be adults who either experience such a need for approval that they may at times be desolate without it or who feel that they have an inalienable right to be taken care of without effort on their part. The effort to control the child is one extreme which defeats the development of the flexible and creative personality. The other extreme is undue permissiveness, which fosters dependency, a lack of self-discipline, and an inability to appreciate limits, which make any kind of genuine accomplishment very difficult.

Creativity is fostered in chidren by a parental attitude that simultaneously permits them to express themselves freely in words and at play and sets clearly defined limits that preclude destructive or violent actions toward people and things. There is a time to eat and a time to go to bed. There are rules to be followed, but within the framework of an environment that allows personality to develop. However simplistic it may sound, play is an essential part of such growth, for through play children establish a basic sense of their own worth and an acceptance of spontaneity. "Through play," says Hogan, "the infant develops a sense of wholeness and of his own powers, and he must extend this into relationships with others. . . . Play is a way of adapting to changes, of testing oneself in a situation that is new by insuring that one will not fail the test."

Such assurances are not always available later in life. Quite the contrary. With the divorce rate breaking the million-a-year mark, family life is clearly in trouble. Making the family a more creative unit will not only strengthen and improve the quality of the bonds that tie its members together, but it will help to provide an atmosphere in which each can help the others withstand the stresses of a perplexing society and discover, or rediscover, a personal sense of purpose and direction.

13
A Sense
of Direction

We have come full circle, and I am again reminded of
Teilhard de Chardin's thesis that we are engaged in a
crucial phase of human evolution—crucial because it is
characterized by a fundamental expansion in consciousness. Implicit in what he proposed is an expansion in individual freedom. Some time ago I read a newspaper edito-
rial which dealt with the subject of freedom, and I saved
it. It did not tie in with a news story but seemed to be
something that the editor felt needed to be written. "Liberty seems inseparable from the concept of individualism.
Only in nations where men and women think of themselves—in some sense and at whatever psychic cost—at
arm's length from the societies in which they dwell does
liberty have room to breathe."

Freedom does not mean total isolation. A plant cannot
grow without being rooted somewhere. The conditions
under which the plant grows—air, moisture, soil—cannot
be inimical to its survival. Walking through the streets of

New York, one occasionally passes an empty lot where some building has been torn down to make room for a new one; because the developer has failed to raise his mortgage money or thinks the market is not right, the space remains unused, and it is possible to see a mass of vegetation pushing out of the ground through the debris in stark defiance of a blanket of concrete. Plants and trees have a strong determination to survive, and their destiny is predetermined by their very nature. Unlike us, they have no choice in the matter. Given the slightest opportunity, they must fulfill their purpose.

For better or worse, human beings have a choice, and therein lies the problem that freedom presents—the issue of personal destiny. It is a matter that we seldom find time to consider, pressed as we are with the details of day-to-day life. We normally leave it to others to answer for us. We are much too busy fixing dinner, wondering how we will pay our bills, worrying about the security of our jobs, trying to figure out how much the other guy has, to give thought to what seems like a remote abstraction. Yet this issue is the cornerstone of the liberty we so violently demand. "There is no liberty," wrote Antoine de Saint-Exupéry in *Flight to Arras*, "except the liberty of some one making his way towards something."

This sense of purpose is a characteristic of the creative person. It comes from many different sources, some within, some without. It is a product of insight, even if such self-knowledge is largely intuitive and never becomes formulated into a logical train of analysis. It is an inherent part of the unique set of circumstances, including genetic inheritance, that separates each of us from everyone else in the universe and gives us our own special identity. Millions of other men and women may be engaged in doing many of the same things that we do—raising children, going to school, feeding information into a computer, making business deals, selling automobiles or Avon products. What we are doing is also a part of our destiny, but our activities derive meaning primarily from how closely they relate to that which is special within us.

Rather than being an idealistic position, this is a highly pragmatic one. If health—mental or physical well-being—depends on a proper equilibrium between ourselves and our environment and among the various psychological and biological forces within us, then the more we live in harmony with what and who we are, the more valid our lives will be. This is merely a restatement of the old expression, "a square peg in a round hole." A woman who is not by nature nurturing, for example, must come to terms with this fact and deal with it before she damages her children and herself. She can marry a man who can compensate for her lack with his own sense of parenthood. She can choose not to have children. She can try to cultivate this trait in herself. She can work outside her home and have a mother's helper or a day-care center provide her children with this necessary ingredient for their growth. She has a number of options available to her, but only if she knows her potential and limitations, understands the various alternatives, and intentionally chooses the one which will best suit her circumstances.

The emphasis that Rollo May put on the role of courage in the creative process is well deserved. As simple as it sounds, to go through the steps of facing yourself and your life situation and doing something to improve things requires courage, because it involves confronting, quite consciously, the fear of disturbing the current state of equilibrium in which you exist, even when you are slowly going under by keeping things as they are. Patients who consult psychiatrists can often look back years to turning points when the life pattern in which they found themselves no longer worked for them, but they frankly admit that they could not motivate themselves to do anything about it, even to acknowledge the problems, until the hurting became so intense that they no longer had any choice in the matter. There is a need to hold on, to maintain the status quo.

I remember, during the economic depression of the 1930s, the epidemic of fear that not only spread among those who were actually threatened with no food on the table but also affected those who were relatively secure financially, because they were afraid of losing any part of what they had come to possess. This kind of clinging, often confused with hoarding or selfishness, is, in fact, though externalized and tangibly experienced, rooted in a fear of coming apart inside. It is an example of the way fear can not only block an accurate appraisal of reality but also severely limit one's freedom to consider a situation in any new creative way.

How does a psychiatrist regard the patient who has spent years in a futile effort to cope with distress or, worse yet, has reached out for help from a variety of sources, professional and otherwise, and still not been able to resolve his or her problems? If the psychiatrist views the patient's unhappiness and the complications it has caused as a piece of bad luck or misdirection, there is not much to be said. On the other hand, if the psychiatrist considers the possibility that it was somehow "meant" to be this way, is this only the kind of post-hoc rationalization that we are all tempted to use from time to time to explain disappointments—the kind of explanation expressed in "Dad wouldn't let me use the car, but then, maybe if he did, I would have been in an accident"? Or is the therapist in touch with the delicate balance that exists between self-determination and personal destiny?

"The real task," wrote Saint-Exupéry, "is to succeed in setting man free by making him master of himself." These are vital words in this age of homogenization, but they tell only half the story. In seeming contradiction to this point of view is that posed by others—that of Alan Watts, for example: "People try to force issues only when not realizing that it can't be done . . . there is no way of deviating from the watercourse of nature." Boldness and choice on the one hand, fate on the other.

The possibility of a force operating in the lives of each of us that could properly be called destiny struck me some years ago. At that time I was working in therapy with a twenty-eight-year-old woman named Charlotte who had come to me in a serious state of depression after the end of a very unrewarding and more or less one-sided love involvement. It was the last in a series of such relationships that had succeeded one another, with a certain regularity, since she was twenty-two. She had a way of being drawn to men who were at best insensitive, and sometimes frankly cruel. It was as if, scanning the world, she had overlooked the possibility that a relationship could have any other character to it.

At twenty Charlotte had met a member of the faculty at the college she attended who was quite drawn to her, and for the first time she felt a serious interest in a man. He was in his early thirties, unmarried, mature, intelligent, sensitive, and although he kept at a distance during her student years, they began to see a great deal of each other after her graduation. "I wanted to marry him, but when he confronted me with his feeling that there was too great an age difference between us—fourteen years—I felt desperate and broke it off and refused to see him again." After that, she became quite promiscuous for several years. "I found myself sleeping with any boy who'd have me, in spite of the fact that I never had an orgasm. I suppose I wanted to be wanted, in any way, and that was about the most basic way of insuring that I'd be wanted."

A second turning point in Charlotte's life was the death of her father, to whom she had been very attached; he died suddenly, of a coronary, when she was twenty-two. Although the pain subsided, she never fully recovered from the impact of the grief that she experienced then. This grief translated itself into a subtle, persistent state of chronic depression that impeded her spontaneity, rendered her more passive and withdrawn in her social life, and resulted in an inability to reach out toward men in whom she might have been naturally interested while remaining vulnerable to those who pushed aggressively enough to break through her withdrawal.

Toward the end of treatment, which ran over a period of

eight months, Charlotte was no longer depressed, no longer using sex as an outlet for her feelings of self-abnegation and to gain acceptance, no longer berating herself for having made errors in judgment in romantic involvements. But having resolved many of her conflicts about herself in relation to men, she felt herself confronted with a new dilemma: "Now that I feel ready, really ready, to love someone and get married and have children, I feel it's too late. The men I find myself attracted to are already committed, and the others who aren't just don't seem to interest me. And I can't help but think, what's the point in settling your problems if there's no way you can direct the energy and desires that come to the surface once they're settled?"

Four months after the end of her therapy, Charlotte sent me a copy of a letter she had received from the professor she had met during her college years. He had married and had three children, and his wife had died of cancer that past spring. He had left the academic life and was living and working in Geneva, Switzerland, for an agency of the United Nations. He had written to tell her that he would be visiting the United States for a few weeks and wanted to know if he could come and see her. Six months after that, I received an invitation to their wedding and five years later, a Christmas card with a photograph of Charlotte, her three stepchildren, her husband, and two children of their own, postmarked Switzerland and inscribed "With love and gratitude."

It sounds suspiciously like the contrived ending of a television soap opera or a daytime radio serial of the 1930s. It is not. It reflects a reality that I have seen too often to dismiss: namely, that at that point at which a patient has sufficiently resolved his or her environmental and inner problems and is ready to meet the world again with imagination and energy, things fall into place in a way that goes beyond the limitations of the individual's own possible influence. A collaboration occurs between the person and events that begins in his or her own sense of purpose and direction and then seems to enlist the cooperation of what, for lack of a better term, might be called fate.

Carl Jung called this phenomenon "synchronicity." He defined it as "the simultaneous occurrence of two meaningfully but not causally connected events," and to account for it he presumed the existence of some kind of force "equal in rank to causality as a principle of explanation." At the very moment when we are struggling to sustain a sense of personal autonomy, we are also caught up in vital forces that are much larger than ourselves, so that while we may be the protagonists of our own lives, we are the extras or spear carriers in some larger drama. Yet contained within the script of the play is a part, or series of parts, for which we are uniquely suited. Sometimes there seems to be a casting director who assigns us properly. Most of the time we are left to our own devices to discover ways and means of fitting into this larger system so that its movement will reinforce, rather than stifle, our own identities.

The phenomenon sounds mystical only because we do not understand it. But there are innumerable clues available, given the right frame of mind—openness—and the ability to synthesize the clues into a whole.

Choosing a career is an example. In college, I often

envied those students who seemed possessed by a single-
ness of purpose, who had everything all lined up and
planned out. Pulled apart by a wide range of interests and
ambitions and needs, I fluctuated between wanting to be a
doctor at one time, a journalist at another, and a research
scientist at still another. Reading Kenneth Grahame's *The
Wind in the Willows*, as an adult as well as in childhood, I
could always identify both with Toad and his spirit of
reckless adventure and with Mole and his need for security, his realization, on returning to his house in the
ground, of "how plain and simple—how narrow, even—it
all was; but clearly, too, how much it all meant to him,
and the special value of some such anchorage in one's existence."

Not without conflict, I chose medicine as a field in
which all my interests might become integrated with my
own needs as I understood them. It was a painful decision,
even as was the later decision to enter psychiatry as a
specialty. There seemed to be a great deal of forfeiting involved. The choice seemed limiting, a feeling that I experienced more in the heart than in the mind, where logic
kept reminding me that I was making the right decision.

The years that have passed have served to quiet my uncertainty and confirm the correctness of my choice. I have
a sense of faithfulness to something rather deeply ingrained
within my own nature, and a feeling that this is what I
want to do and at the same time what I seem to have been
"meant to do." There is a feeling of moving with myself
and reality rather than of moving against. This momen-
tum has not been without fear or sometimes a feeling of

futility, but it has been characterized by a growing freedom from the all-too-common need to force events.

Nor do I find Jung's concept of synchronicity and its seeming incomprehensibility at all contradictory to the "hard," measurable information that emerges from the scientists' laboratories. If, in all of us, a sense of well-being is dependent on identifying some purpose in life to give it meaning, there is no reason why that cannot translate into specific biological terms—a way of life in which the physiological channels required for the person to accommodate to stressful events, such as shifts in body calcium and hormones, can endure against the process of depletion for a longer period of time. We are psychobiological units. If the ability to fall apart and come back together again is a necessary aspect of the response to stress that requires a redefinition of ourselves, this complex, integrative function clearly demands an intact body as well as an intact mind.

The question remains: To what end shall our mental and physical energies be put? Originality, flexibility, a sense of purpose, the renewed feeling of put-togetherness, periods of contentment and even joy? Once we have achieved these psychological advantages, how will we use them? Or will they automatically move us in some given direction?

Oddly, it came as a surprise to me, in reading various books and articles on creativity, to realize that the creative process could be used for the purpose of sustaining ways of thinking and patterns of behavior that were inherently neurotic and destructive. I had always placed the word "creativity" on the list of terms that have good vibrations—like "freedom" and "hope." By implication, to be more creative could only make you a better person.

Here we run into the problem of definition. If creativity is primarily the ability to look at ideas in new ways or to tie previously contradictory concepts together because of freshly perceived similarities, it actually carries with it no moral force. After all, to devise a heating system that depends on solar energy is no more creative than to have invented the guillotine, which, however malevolent its associations, is a highly effective device in terms of its purpose.

Evil is a very real force, and its "de-emphasis," as Karl Menninger wrote in *The Vital Balance*, "is as unrealistic as the pessimistic conclusion that man is all evil." Not only are we quite capable of activating a destructiveness that lies within us, but we can also move into the orbit of an external reality that is itself inherently destructive. And so the person whose evil tendencies are operating in cooperation with those of an evil environment has, in fact, attained a kind of equilibrium.

What matters is the nature of the balance we achieve. Through insight we can come to distinguish between constructive and destructive forces, within and without. Even knowing that such a distinction is necessary is part of the process of insight. The cultivation of our creative energies can permit us to move in harmony with a universal force for life, with whatever it is that whispers to the seeds in the vacant city lot that it is time to start growing.

In the life of each of us there are usually several points at which, because we have achieved a singular level of success or, more often, have been brought to our knees by a defeat that humiliates, we are uniquely positioned to make choices that will determine for years to come, for the rest of our lives perhaps, which side of the life-death polarity we will find ourselves moving toward. At such times we feel a heady kind of freedom born of accomplishment, or, conversely, the kind of freedom that comes from the hopelessness of having nothing left of what we once valued. It is at these points that we must be ready to make a right choice.

What comes before is really a getting ready. What comes afterward depends upon how ready we are and what choices we make.

Selected Bibliography

Arieti, Sylvano. *Creativity: The Magic Synthesis.* New York: Basic Books, 1976.

Becker, Ernest. *The Denial of Death.* New York: The Free Press, 1973.

Bronowski, Jacob. "The Creative Process," Scientific American, vol. 199 (1958), pp. 59–65.

Butler, Samuel. *The Way of All Flesh.* New York: Dutton, 1903.

Campbell, Joseph. *The Hero with a Thousand Faces.* New York: Pantheon Books, 1949.

Charlton, Randolph S. "Creativity and Sexuality." *Creative Psychiatry.* New York: Life Sciences Advisory Group/Geigy Pharmaceuticals, 1976.

Erikson, Erik H. *Childhood and Society.* New York: Norton, 1950.

Flach, Frederic F. *The Secret Strength of Depression.* New York: Lippincott, 1974.

———. "The Creative Process in Psychiatry." *Creative Psychiatry.* New York: Life Sciences Advisory Group/Geigy Pharmaceuticals, 1975.

————, and Draghi, Suzanne, eds. *The Nature and Treatment of Depression*. New York: Wiley, 1975.

Freud, Sigmund. "A Note on the Unconscious in Psycho-Analysis" (1912). *Collected Papers: Volume IV*. New York: Basic Books, 1959.

Friedman, Meyer, and Rosenman, Ray H. *Type A Behavior and Your Heart*. New York: Knopf, 1975.

Ghiselin, Brewster. *The Creative Process*. Berkeley, Calif.: University of California Press, 1952.

Grahame, Kenneth. *The Wind in the Willows*. New York: Scribners, 1933.

Henderson, D. K. *Psychopathic States*. New York: Norton, 1939.

Hogan, Peter. "Creativity in the Family." *Creative Psychiatry*. New York: Life Sciences Advisory Group/Geigy Pharmaceuticals, 1975.

Huxley, Aldous. *The Doors of Perception*. New York: Harper & Brothers, 1954.

Jay, Anthony. *Management and Machiavelli*. New York: Holt, Rinehart & Winston, 1968.

Jones, Ernest. *The Life and Work of Sigmund Freud*. 3 vols. New York: Basic Books, 1953, 1955, 1957.

Kees, Weldon. *The Collected Poems of Weldon Kees*. Lincoln, Nebr.: University of Nebraska Press, 1975.

Koestler, Arthur. *The Roots of Coincidence*. New York: Random House, 1972.

————. *Act of Creation*. New York: MacMillan, 1974.

Kubie, Lawrence. *Neurotic Distortion of the Creative Process*. Lawrence, Kans.: University of Kansas Press, 1958.

Laing, R. D. *The Divided Self*. Baltimore: Penguin Books, 1965.

Lorenz, Konrad. *Civilized Man's Eight Deadly Sins*. New York: Harcourt Brace Jovanovich, 1974.

Marris, Peter. *Loss and Change*. New York: Pantheon Books, 1974.

May, Rollo. *The Courage to Create.* New York: Norton, 1975.

McCully, Robert S. "Contributions of Jungian Psychotherapy Toward Understanding the Creative Process." *Creative Psychiatry.* New York: Life Sciences Advisory Group/Geigy Pharmaceuticals, 1975.

Menninger, Karl. *Theory of Psychoanalytic Technique.* New York: Basic Books, 1958.

————. *The Vital Balance.* New York: Viking, 1963.

Parnes, Sidney J. "Group Creativity." *Creative Psychiatry.* New York: Life Sciences Advisory Group/Geigy Pharmaceuticals, 1976.

Pickering, George. *Creative Malady.* New York: Oxford University Press, 1974.

Reich, Wilhelm. *Character Analysis.* New York: Orgone Institute Press, 1949.

Saint-Exupéry, Antoine de. *Flight to Arras.* New York: Reynal & Hitchcock, 1942.

Sayers, Dorothy L. *The Mind of the Maker.* New York: Harcourt, Brace, 1942.

Schubert, Daniel. "Creativity and the Ability to Cope." *Creative Psychiatry.* New York: Life Sciences Advisory Group/Geigy Pharmaceuticals, 1976.

Seeley, John. *The Americanization of the Unconscious.* New York: Science House, 1967.

Selye, Hans. *The Stress of Life.* New York: McGraw-Hill, 1956.

Skinner, B. F. *Beyond Freedom and Dignity.* New York: Knopf, 1971.

Stein, Morris. *Stimulating Creativity: Vol. 1, Individual Procedures.* New York: Academic Press, 1974.

Steinbeck, John. *The Log from the "Sea of Cortez."* New York: Viking, 1941.

Storr, Anthony. *The Dynamics of Creation.* New York: Atheneum, 1972.

Teilhard de Chardin, Pierre. *The Phenomenon of Man.* New York: Harper & Row, 1959.

Watts, Alan. *Tao: The Watercourse Way.* New York: Pantheon Books, 1975.

Wolf, Stewart, and Wolff, Harold G. *Human Gastric Function: An Experimental Study of Man and His Stomach.* New York: Oxford University Press, 1943.

Index